Disney MARY POPPINS RETURNS

MUSIC FROM THE MOTION PICTURE SOUNDTRACK

ISBN 978-1-5400-4754-0

Walt Disney Music Company

Visit Hal Leonard Online at
www.halleonard.com

Contact us:
Hal Leonard
7777 West Bluemound Road
Milwaukee, WI 53213
Email: info@halleonard.com

In Europe, contact:
Hal Leonard Europe Limited
42 Wigmore Street
Marylebone, London, W1U 2RN
Email: info@halleonardeurope.com

In Australia, contact:
Hal Leonard Australia Pty. Ltd.
4 Lentara Court
Cheltenham, Victoria, 3192 Australia
Email: info@halleonard.com.au

Can You Imagine That?

Registration 2
Rhythm: 2-Beat or Broadway

Music by Marc Shaiman
Lyrics by Scott Wittman
and Marc Shaiman

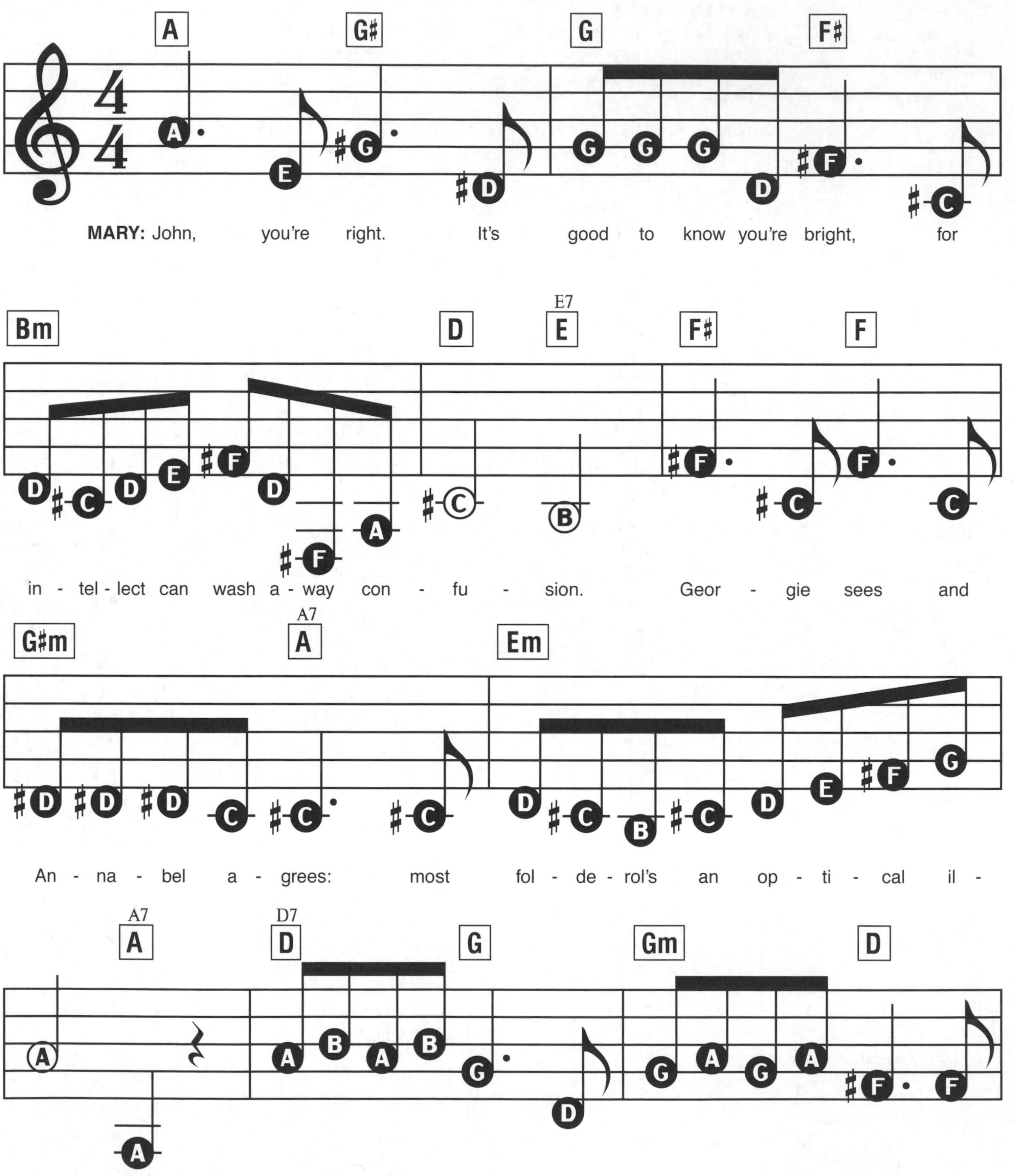

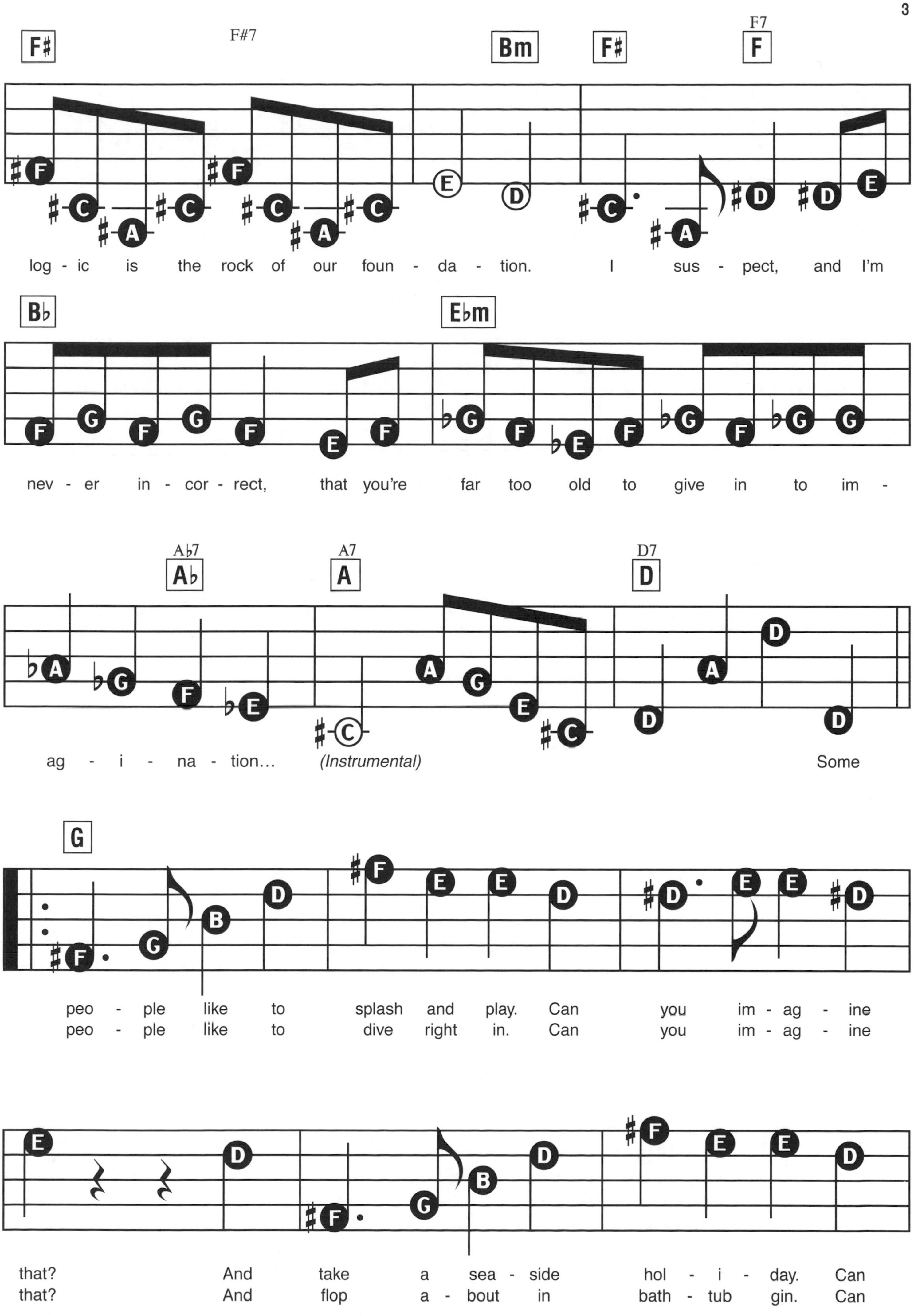

F♯ F#7 Bm F♯ F7 F

log - ic is the rock of our foun - da - tion. I sus - pect, and I'm

B♭ E♭m

nev - er in - cor - rect, that you're far too old to give in to im -

A♭7 A♭ A7 A D7 D

ag - i - na - tion... *(Instrumental)* Some

G

peo - ple like to splash and play. Can you im - ag - ine
peo - ple like to dive right in. Can you im - ag - ine

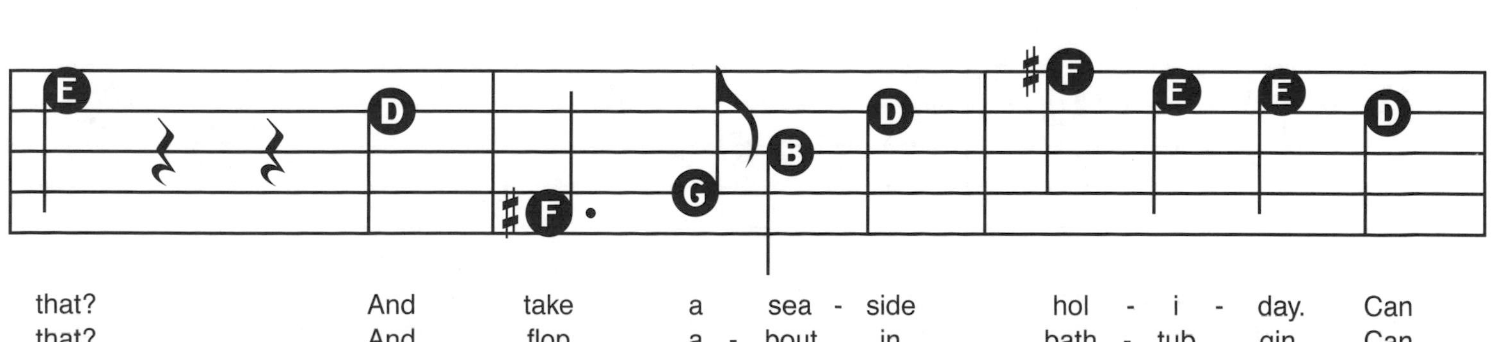
that? And take a sea - side hol - i - day. Can
that? And flop a - bout in bath - tub gin. Can

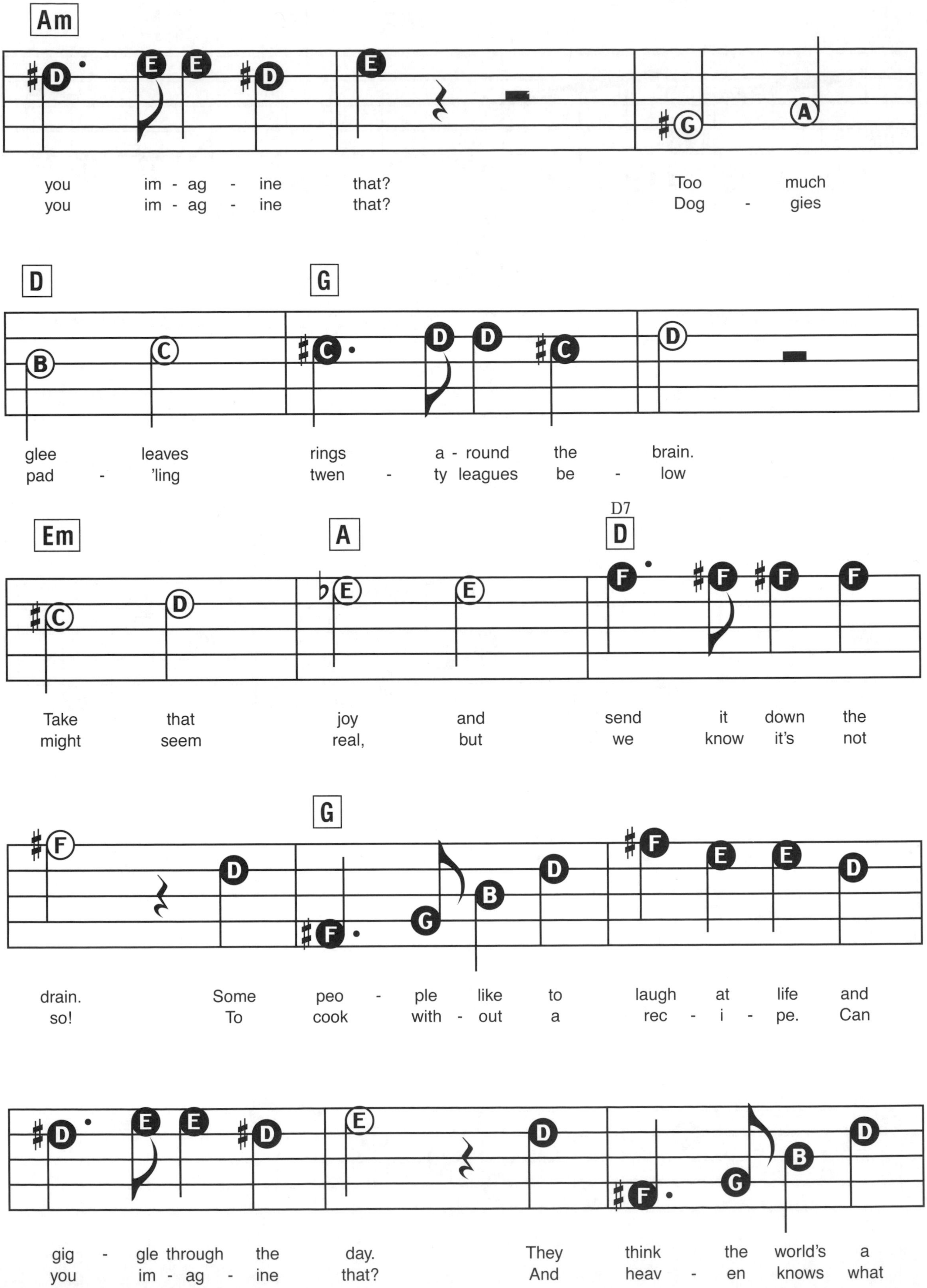

Am

you im - ag - ine that? Too much
you im - ag - ine that? Dog - gies

D G

glee leaves rings a - round the brain.
pad - 'ling twen - ty leagues be - low

Em A D7 D

Take that joy and send it down the
might seem real, but we know it's not

G

drain. Some peo - ple like to laugh at life and
so! To cook with - out a rec - i - pe. Can

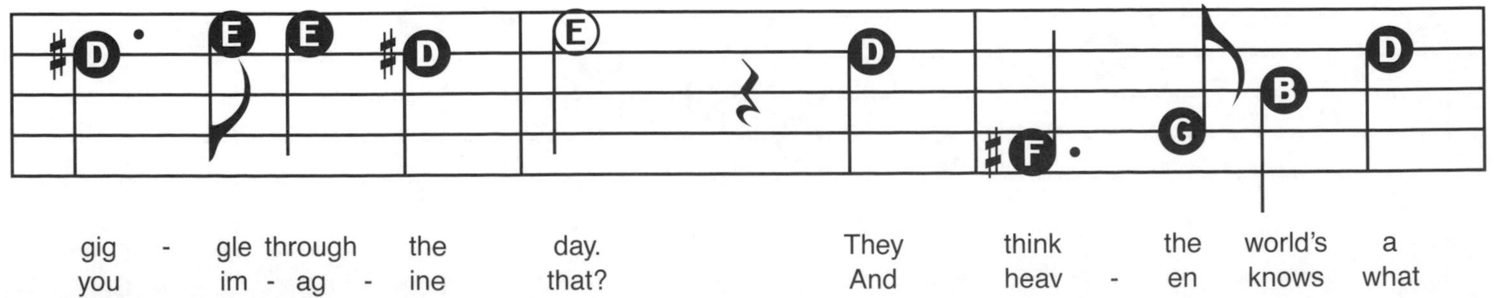
gig - gle through the day. They think the world's a
you im - ag - ine that? And heav - en knows what

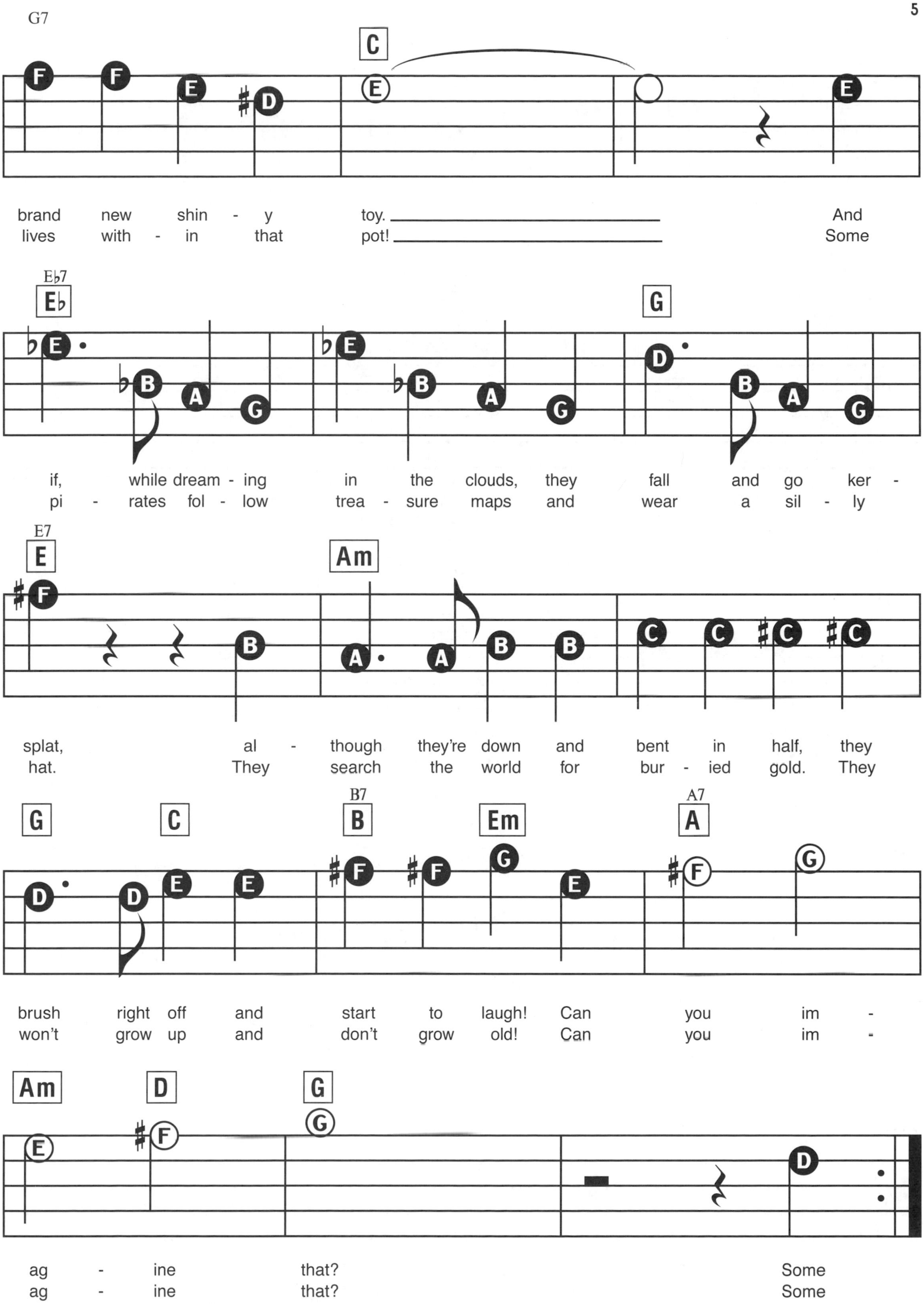

G7 C

brand new shin - y toy. ________ And
lives with - in that pot! ________ Some

Eb7 Eb G

if, while dream - ing in the clouds, they fall and go ker -
pi - rates fol - low trea - sure maps and wear a sil - ly

E7 E Am

splat, al - though they're down and bent in half, they
hat. They search the world for bur - ied gold. They

G C B7 B Em A7 A

brush right off and start to laugh! Can you im -
won't grow up and don't grow old! Can you im -

Am D G

ag - ine that? Some
ag - ine that? Some

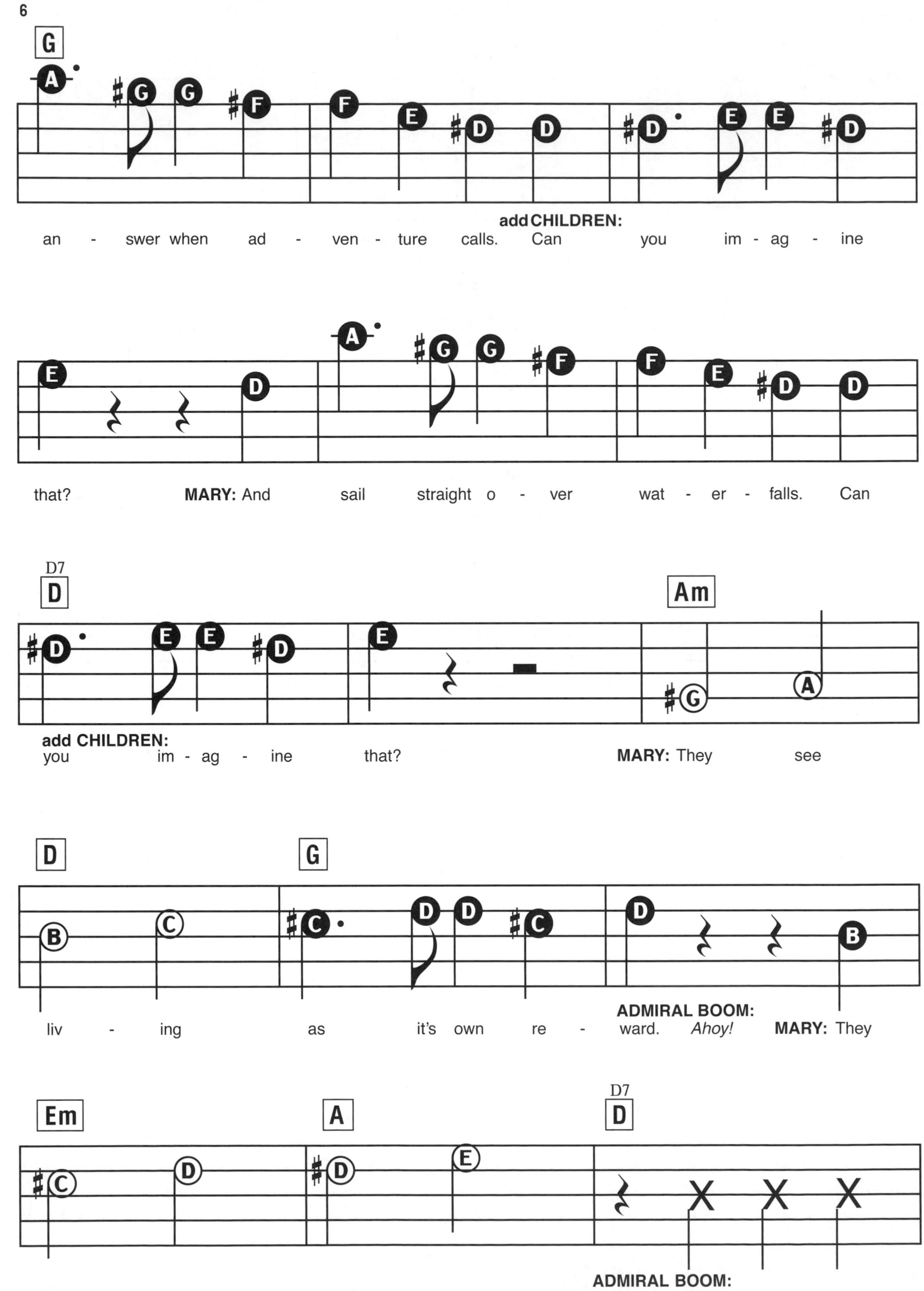
G
an - swer when ad - ven - ture calls.
add CHILDREN:
Can you im - ag - ine
that?
MARY: And sail straight o - ver wat - er - falls. Can
D7
D
Am
add CHILDREN:
you im - ag - ine that?
MARY: They see
D
G
liv - ing as it's own re - ward.
ADMIRAL BOOM:
Ahoy!
MARY: They
Em
A
D7
D
rock the boat, then:
ADMIRAL BOOM:
..."man o - ver

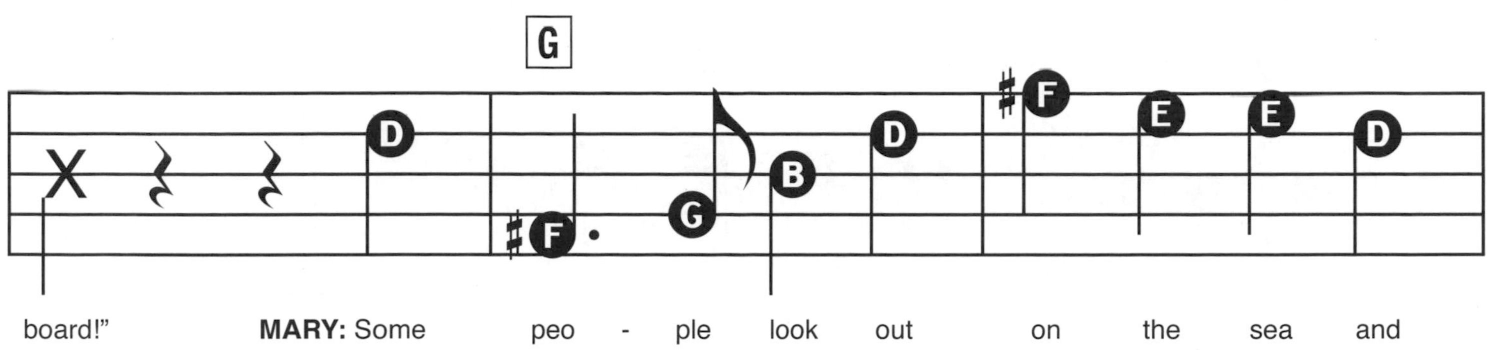
G
board!" MARY: Some peo - ple look out on the sea and

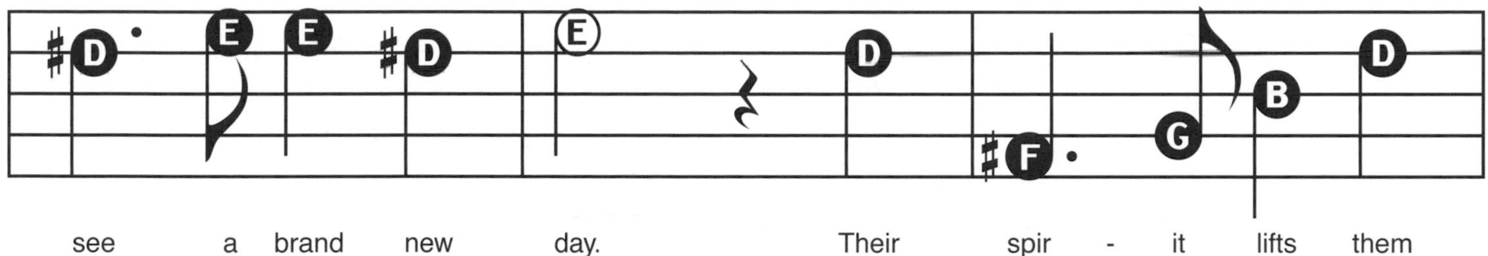
see a brand new day. Their spir - it lifts them

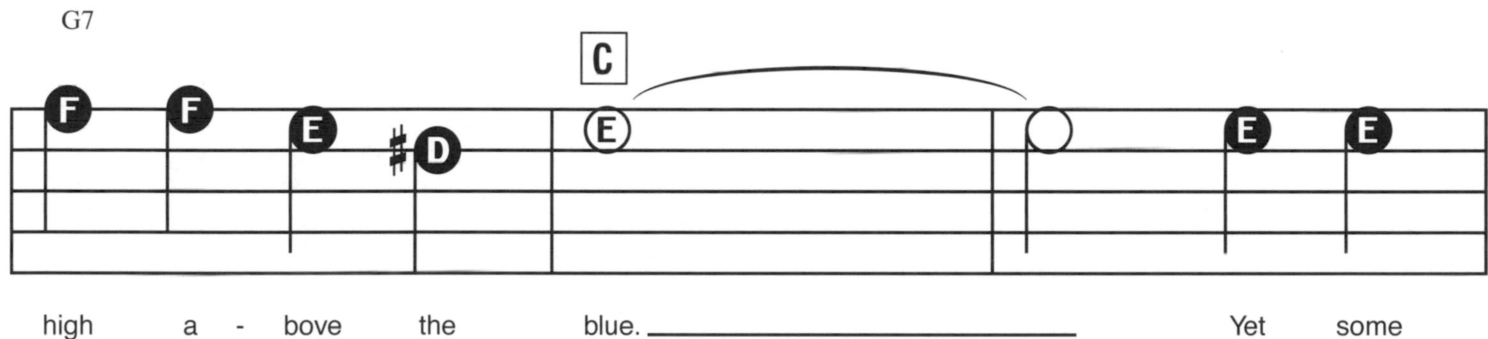
G7
C
high a - bove the blue. Yet some

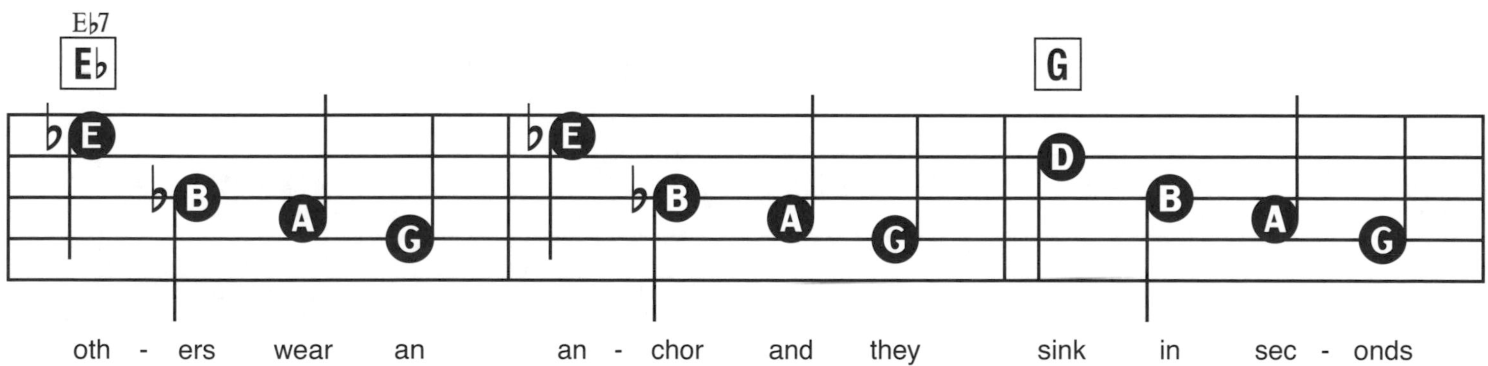
E♭7
E♭
G
oth - ers wear an an - chor and they sink in sec - onds

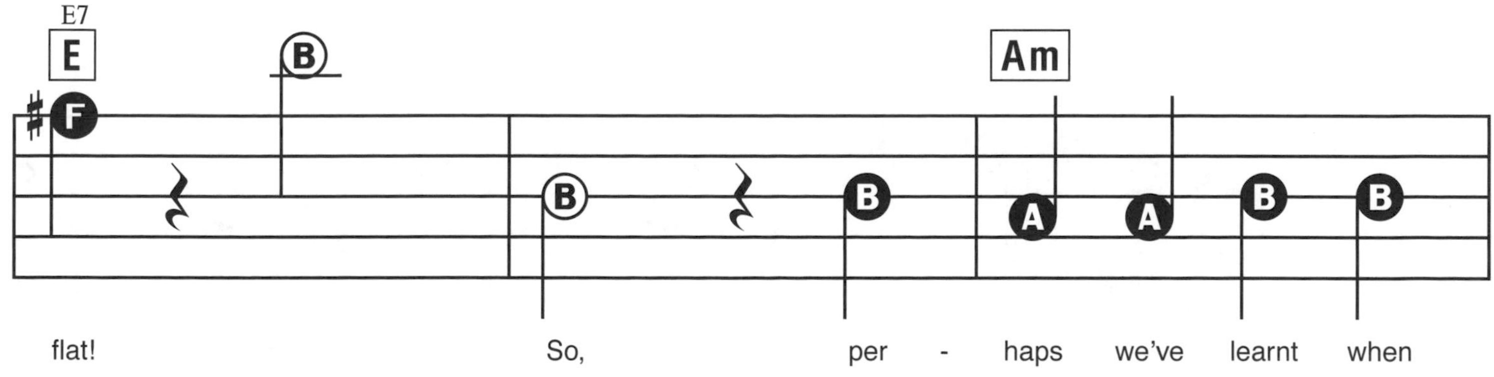
E7
E
Am
flat! So, per - haps we've learnt when

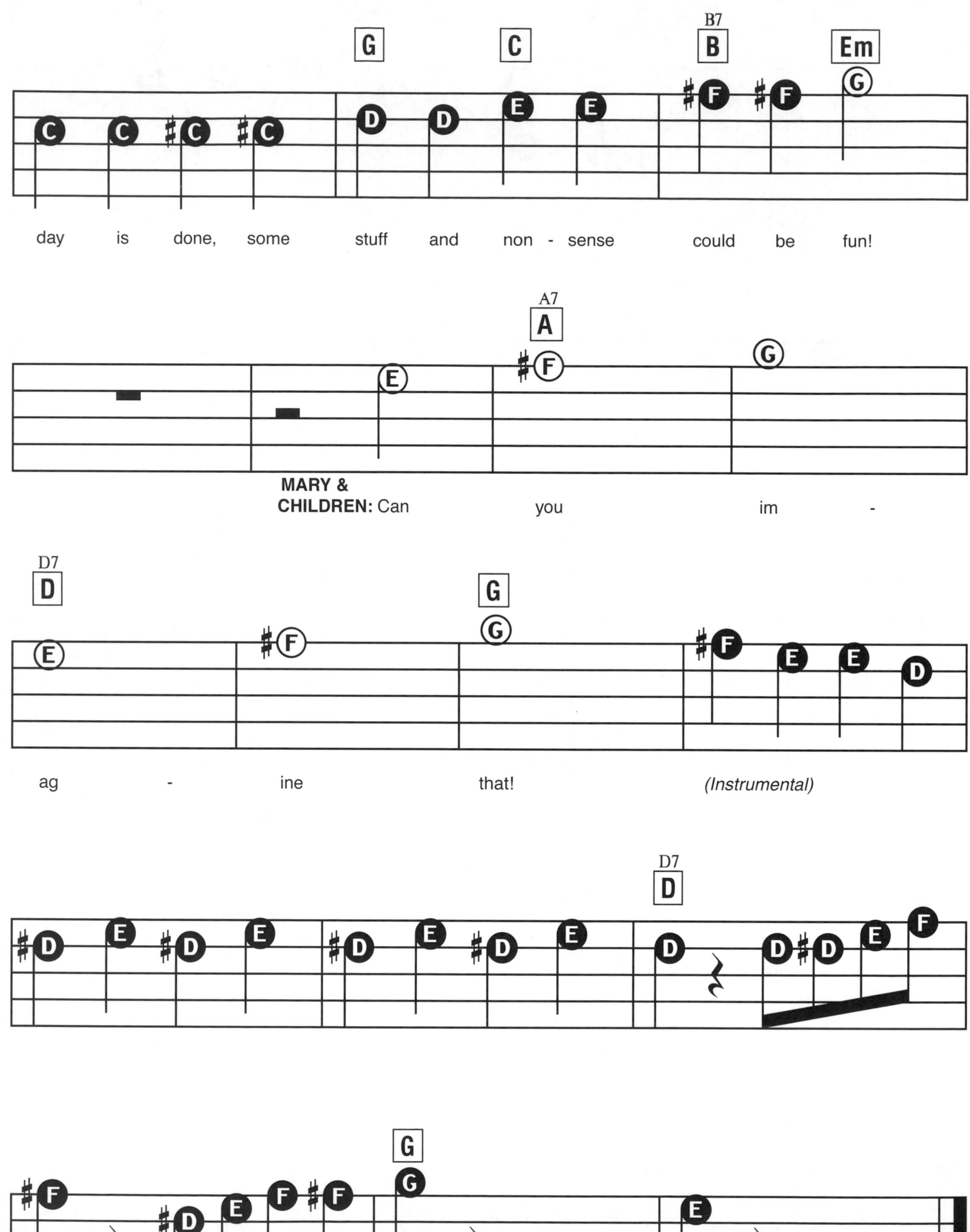
G C B7 B Em
day is done, some stuff and non - sense could be fun!
A7 A
MARY & CHILDREN: Can you im -
D7 D G
ag - ine that!
(Instrumental)
D7 D
G

The Place Where Lost Things Go

Registration 2
Rhythm: Ballad

Music by Marc Shaiman
Lyrics by Scott Wittman
and Marc Shaiman

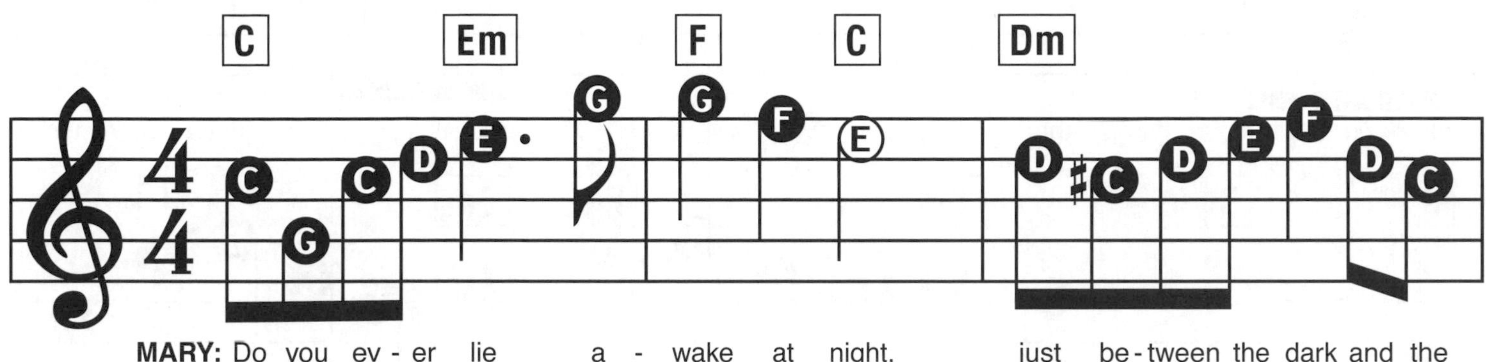
C
Em
F
C
Dm
C G C D E G
G F E
D C D E F D C
MARY: Do you ev - er lie a - wake at night, just be-tween the dark and the

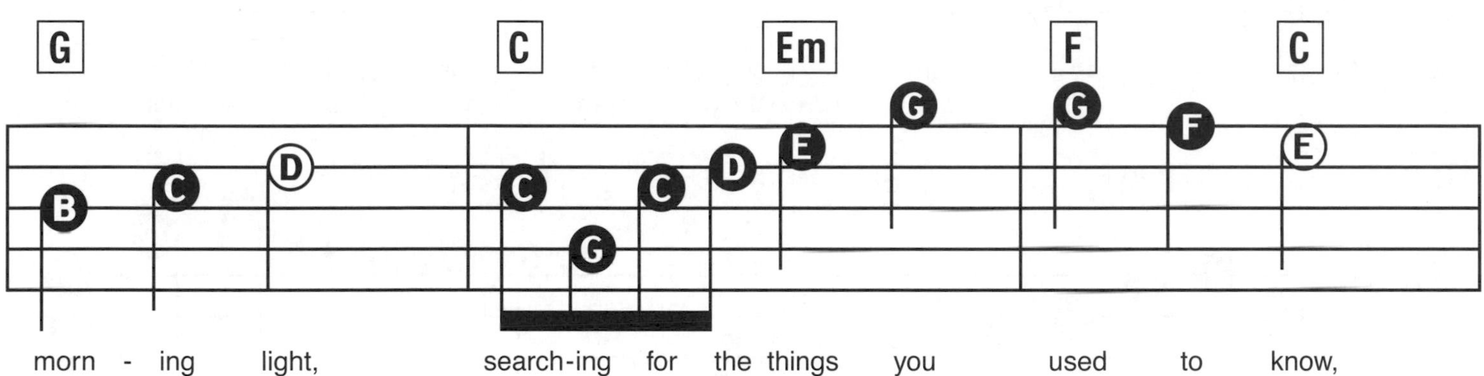
G
C
Em
F
C
B C D
C G C D E G
G F E
morn - ing light, search-ing for the things you used to know,

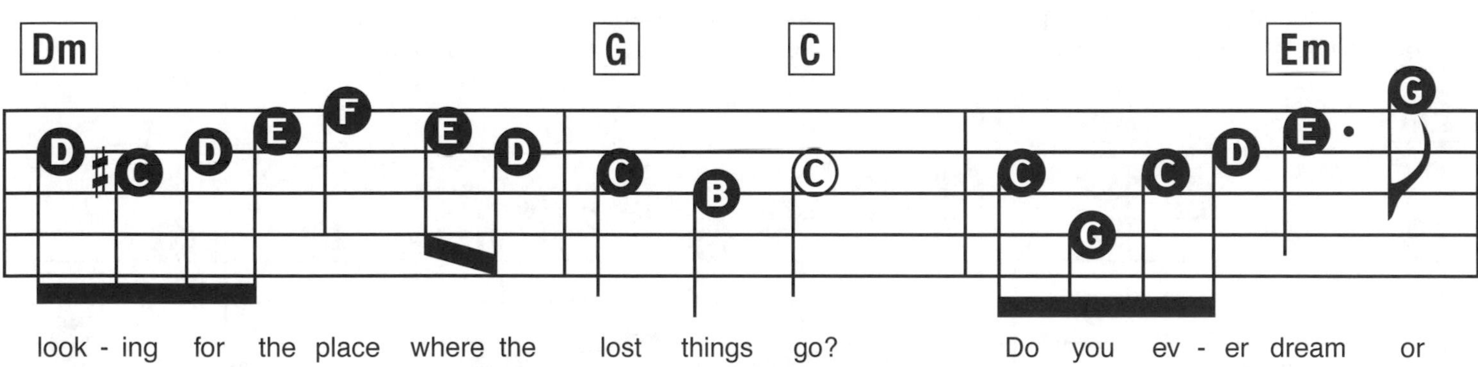
Dm
G
C
Em
D C D E F E D
C B C
C G C D E G
look - ing for the place where the lost things go? Do you ev - er dream or

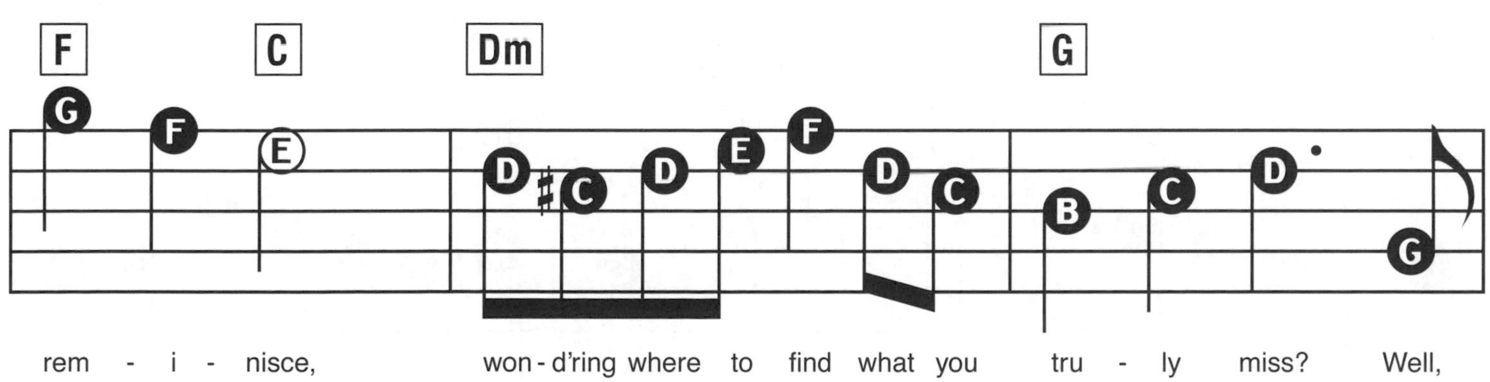
F
C
Dm
G
G F E
D C D E F D C
B C D G
rem - i - nisce, won-d'ring where to find what you tru - ly miss? Well,

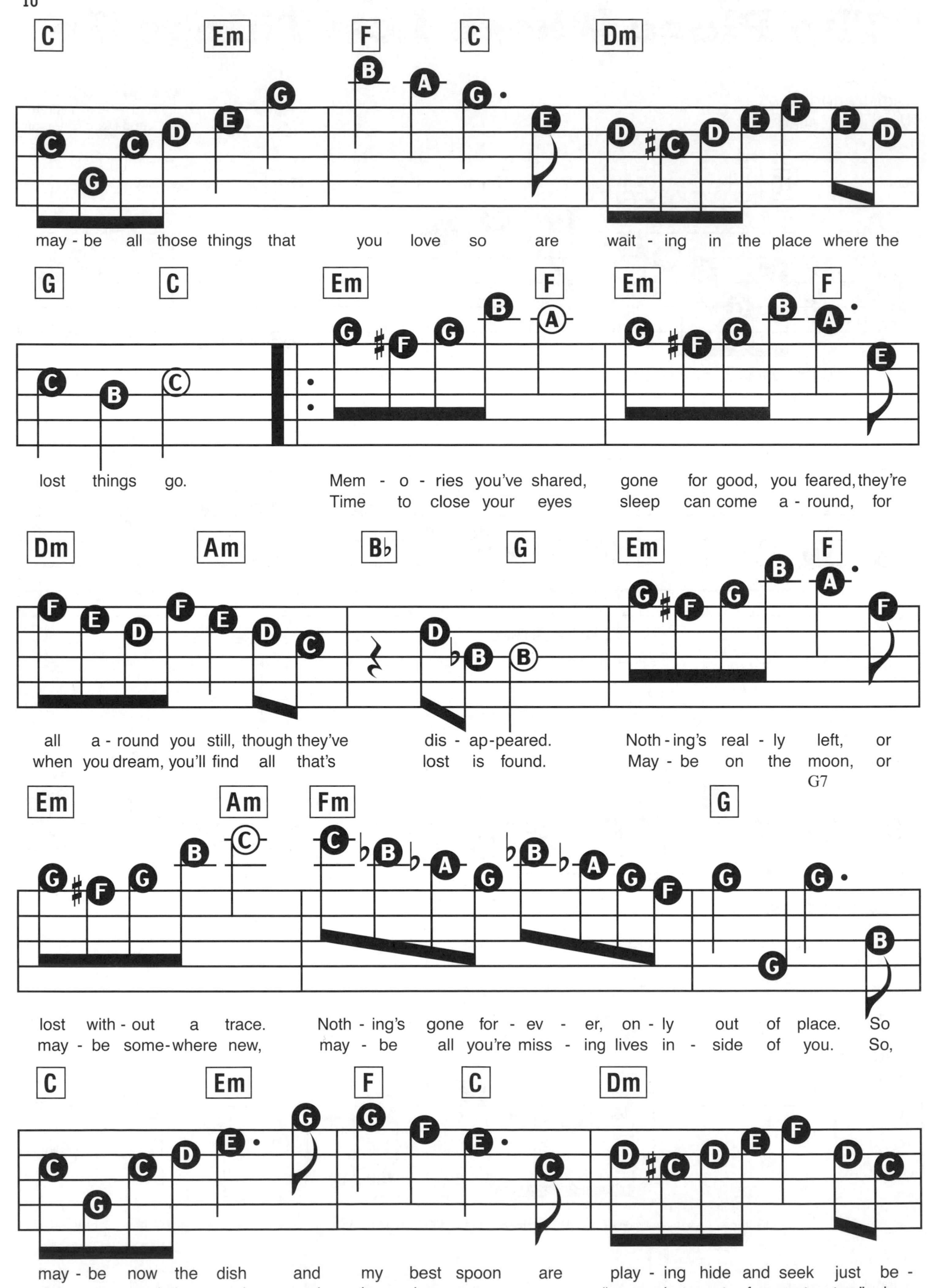
C Em F C Dm
may - be all those things that you love so are wait - ing in the place where the
G C Em F Em F
lost things go.
Mem - o - ries you've shared, gone for good, you feared, they're
Time to close your eyes sleep can come a - round, for
Dm Am B♭ G Em F
all a - round you still, though they've dis - ap - peared. Noth - ing's real - ly left, or
when you dream, you'll find all that's lost is found. May - be on the moon, or
G7
Em Am Fm G
lost with - out a trace. Noth - ing's gone for - ev - er, on - ly out of place. So
may - be some - where new, may - be all you're miss - ing lives in - side of you. So,
C Em F C Dm
may - be now the dish and my best spoon are play - ing hide and seek just be -
when you need her touch and lov - ing gaze, "gone, but not for - got - ten," is

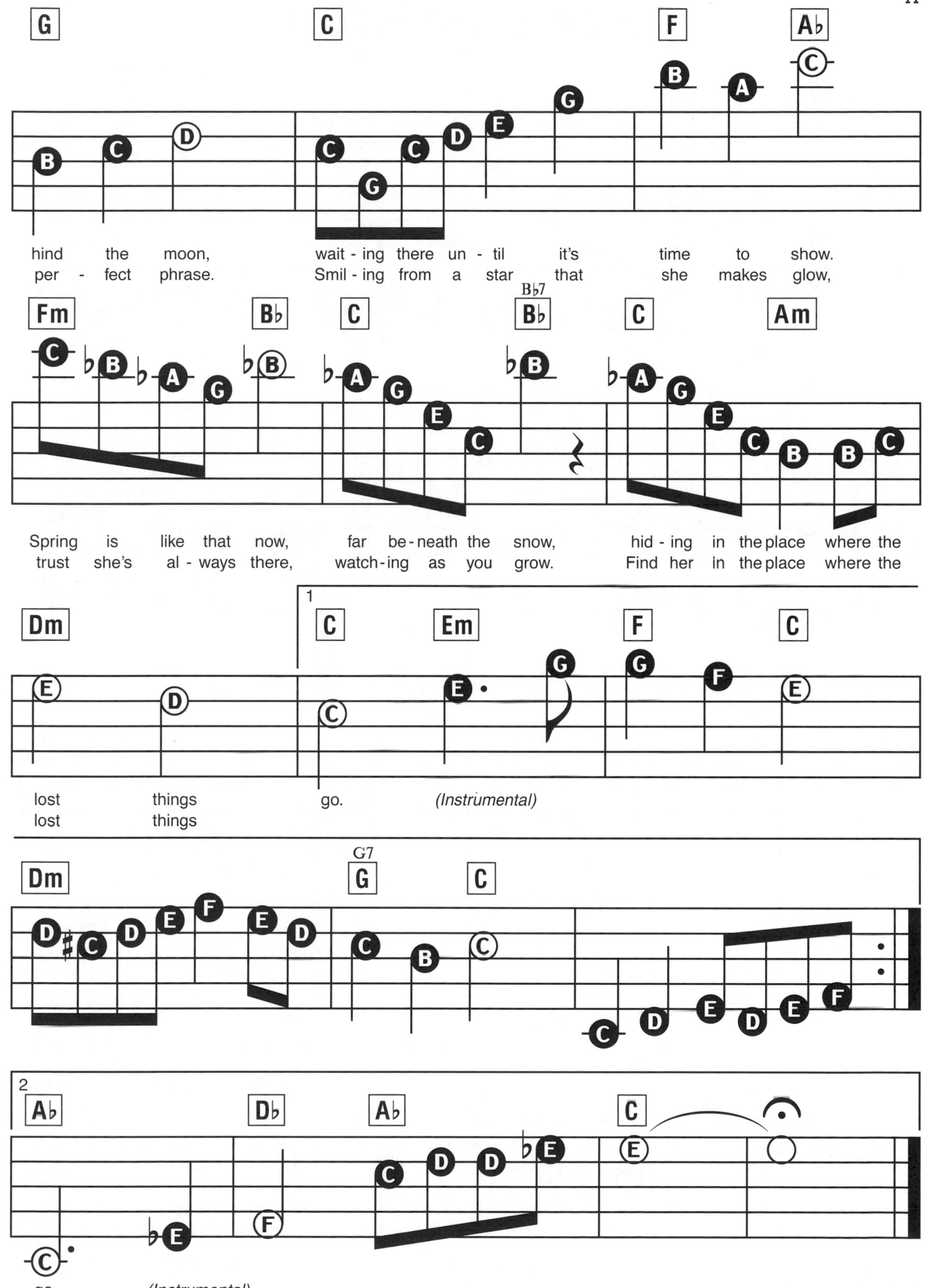
hind the moon, wait - ing there un - til it's time to show.
per - fect phrase. Smil - ing from a star that she makes glow,
Spring is like that now, far be - neath the snow, hid - ing in the place where the
trust she's al - ways there, watch - ing as you grow. Find her in the place where the
lost things go. (Instrumental)
lost things
go. (Instrumental)

A Conversation

Registration 8
Rhythm: None

Music by Marc Shaiman
Lyrics by Scott Wittman
and Marc Shaiman

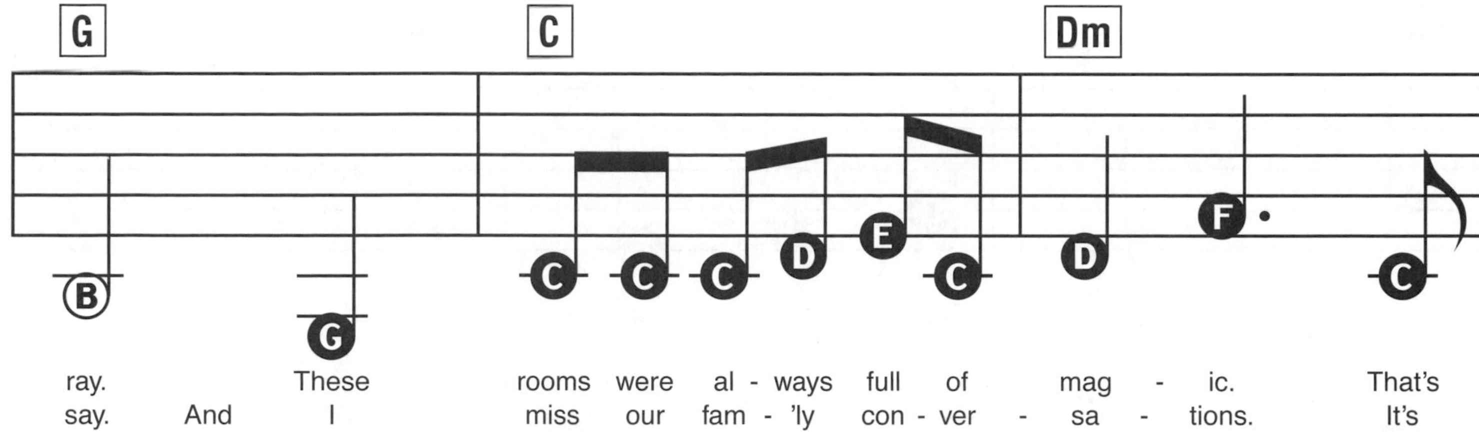
G
C
Dm
B
G
C
C
C
D
E
C
D
F
C
ray. These rooms were al - ways full of mag - ic. That's
say. And I miss our fam - 'ly con - ver - sa - tions. It's

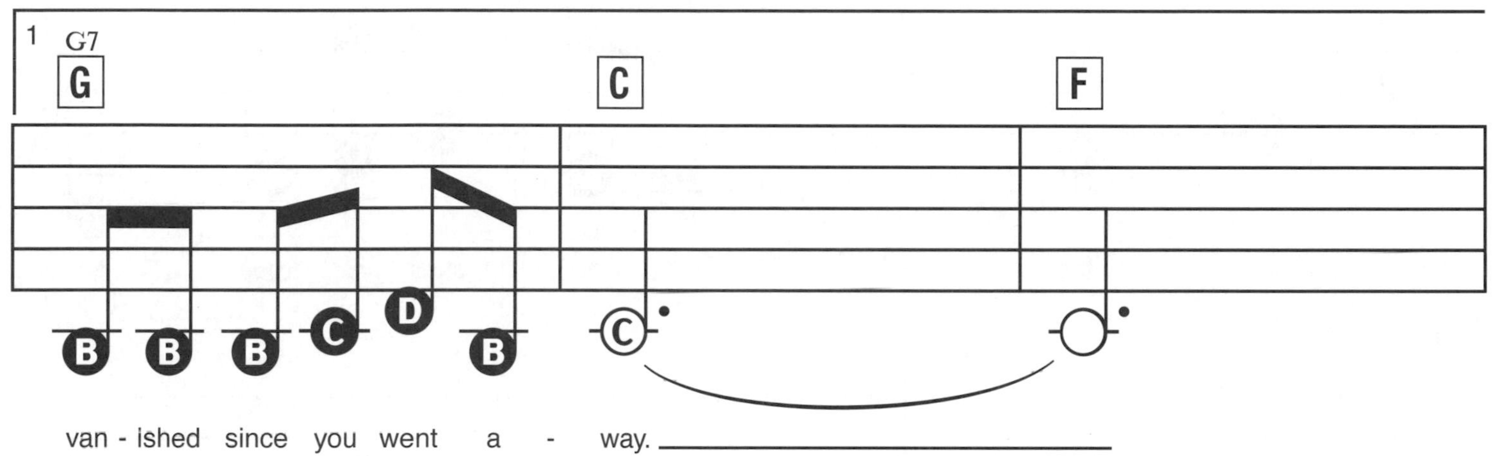
1
G7
G
C
F
B
B
B
C
D
B
C
van - ished since you went a - way.

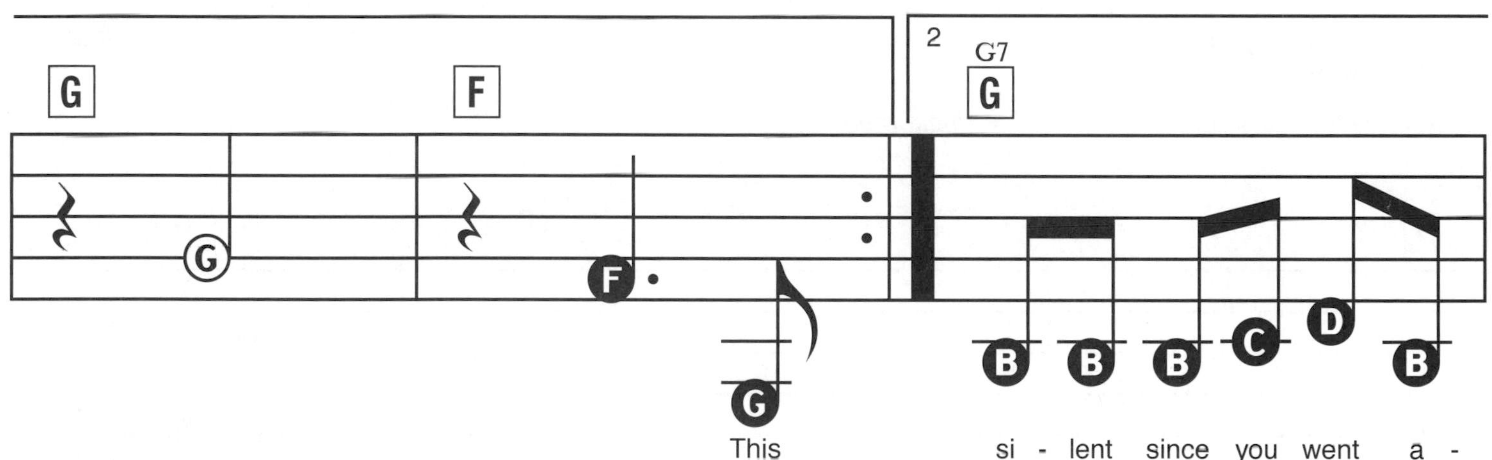
G
F
2
G7
G
G
F
G
B
B
B
C
D
B
This si - lent since you went a -

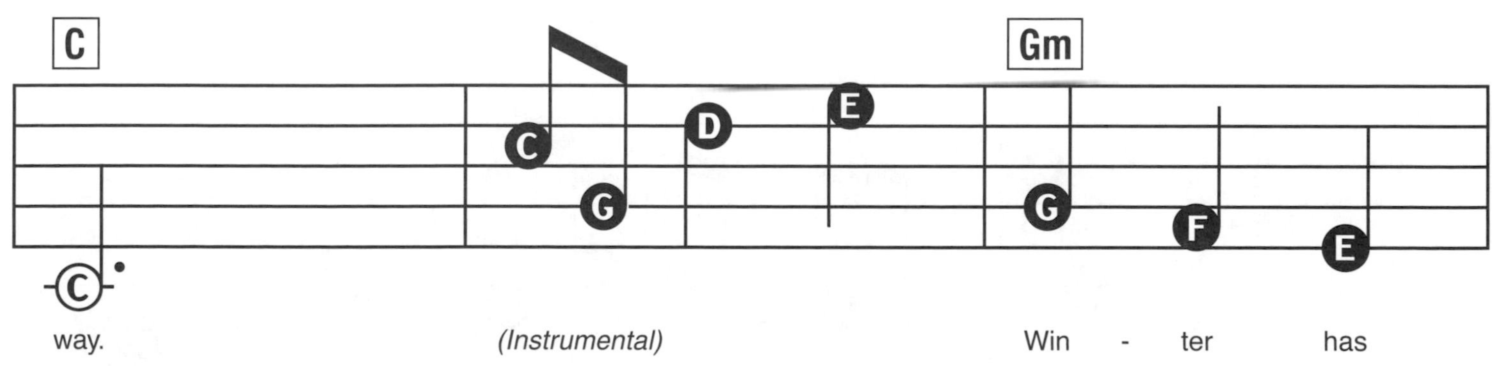
C
Gm
C
C
G
D
E
G
F
E
way. (Instrumental) Win - ter has

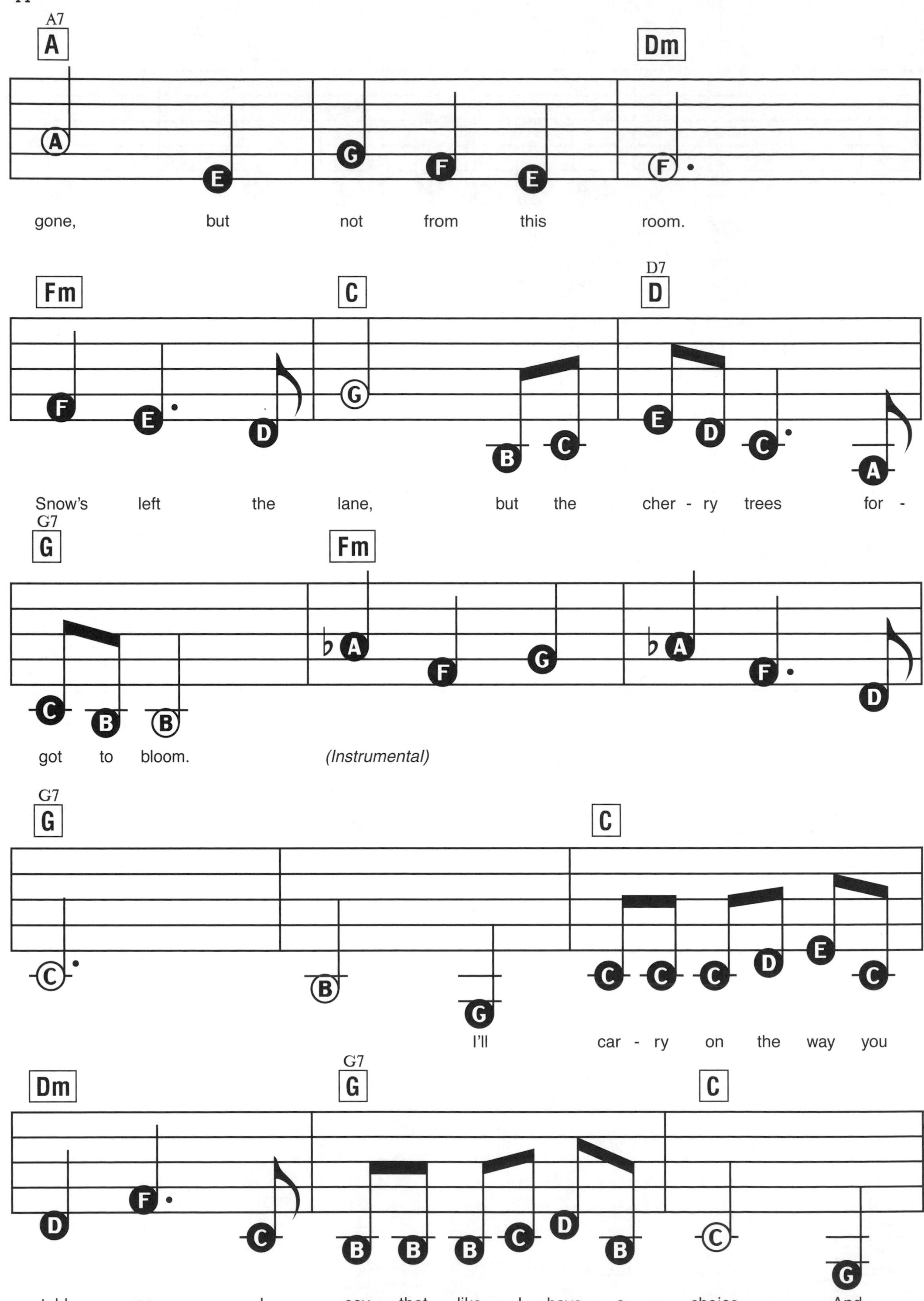
A7
A
Dm
gone, but not from this room.
Fm
C
D7
D
Snow's left the lane, but the cher - ry trees for -
G7
G
Fm
got to bloom.
(Instrumental)
G7
G
C
I'll car - ry on the way you
Dm
G7
G
C
told me. I say that like I have a choice. And

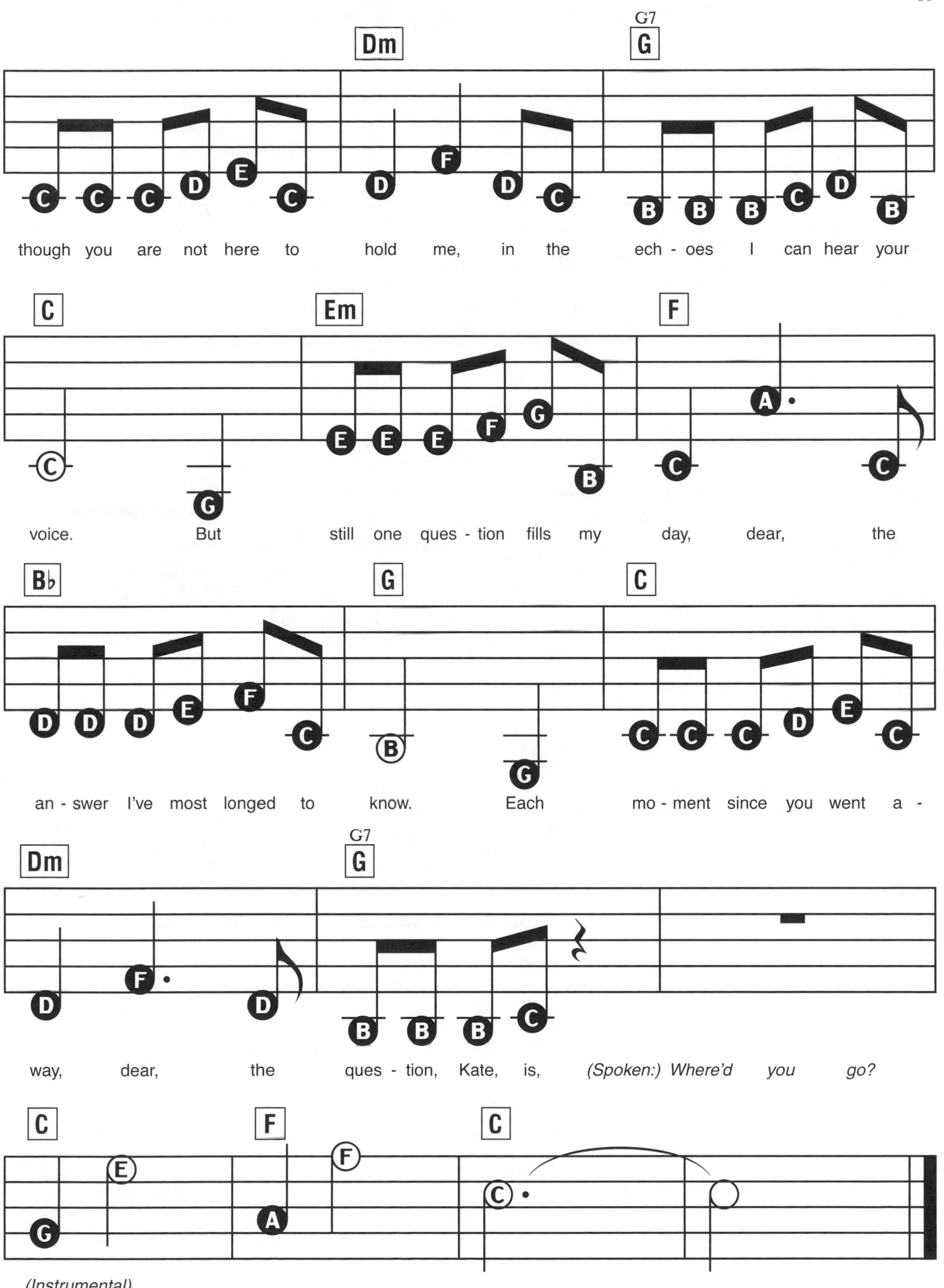
Dm
G7
G
though you are not here to hold me, in the ech - oes I can hear your
C
Em
F
voice. But still one ques - tion fills my day, dear, the
B♭
G
C
an - swer I've most longed to know. Each mo - ment since you went a -
Dm
G7
G
way, dear, the ques - tion, Kate, is, (Spoken:) Where'd you go?
C
F
C
(Instrumental)

A Cover Is Not the Book

Registration 2
Rhythm: None

Music by Marc Shaiman
Lyrics by Scott Wittman
and Marc Shaiman

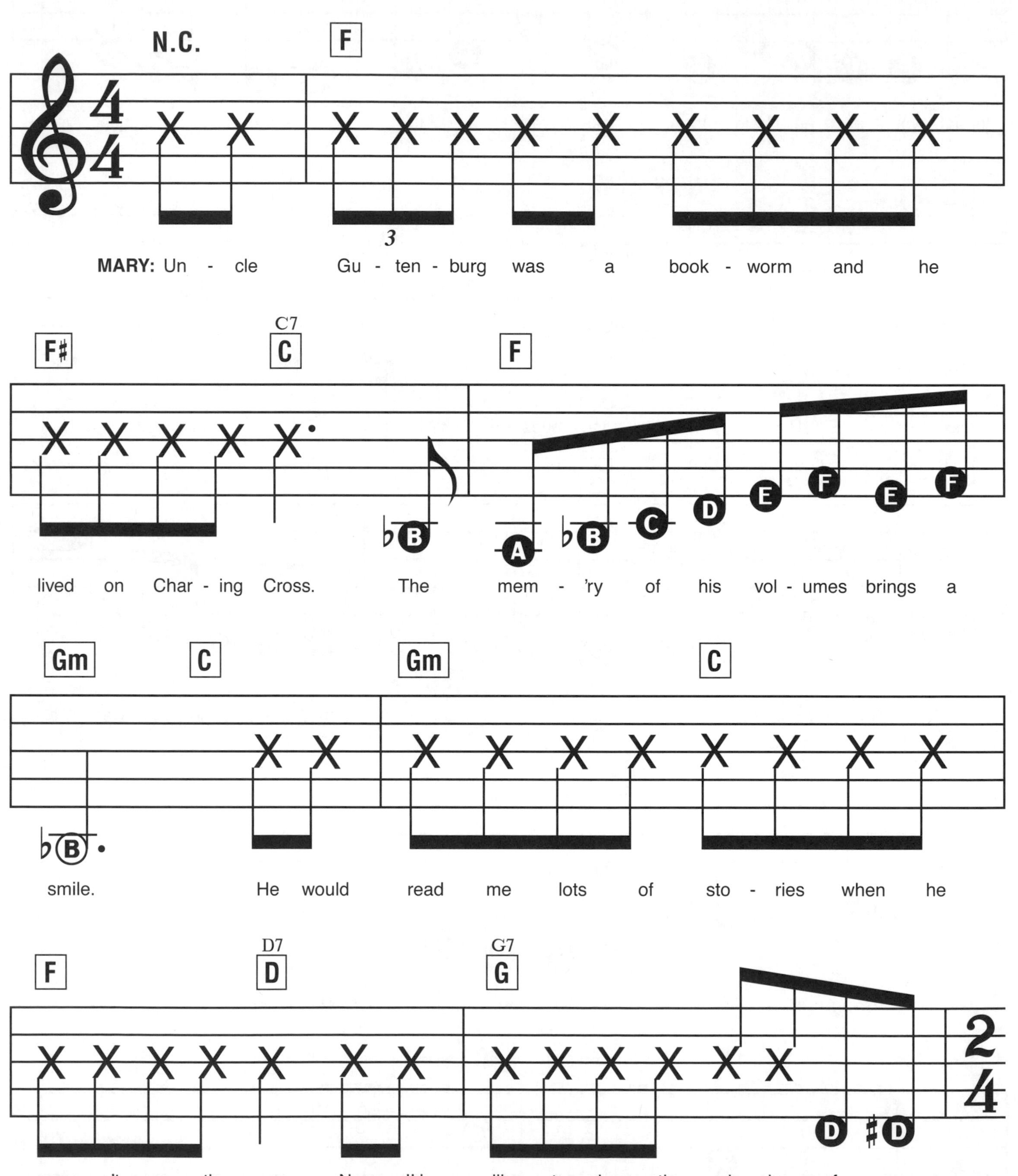

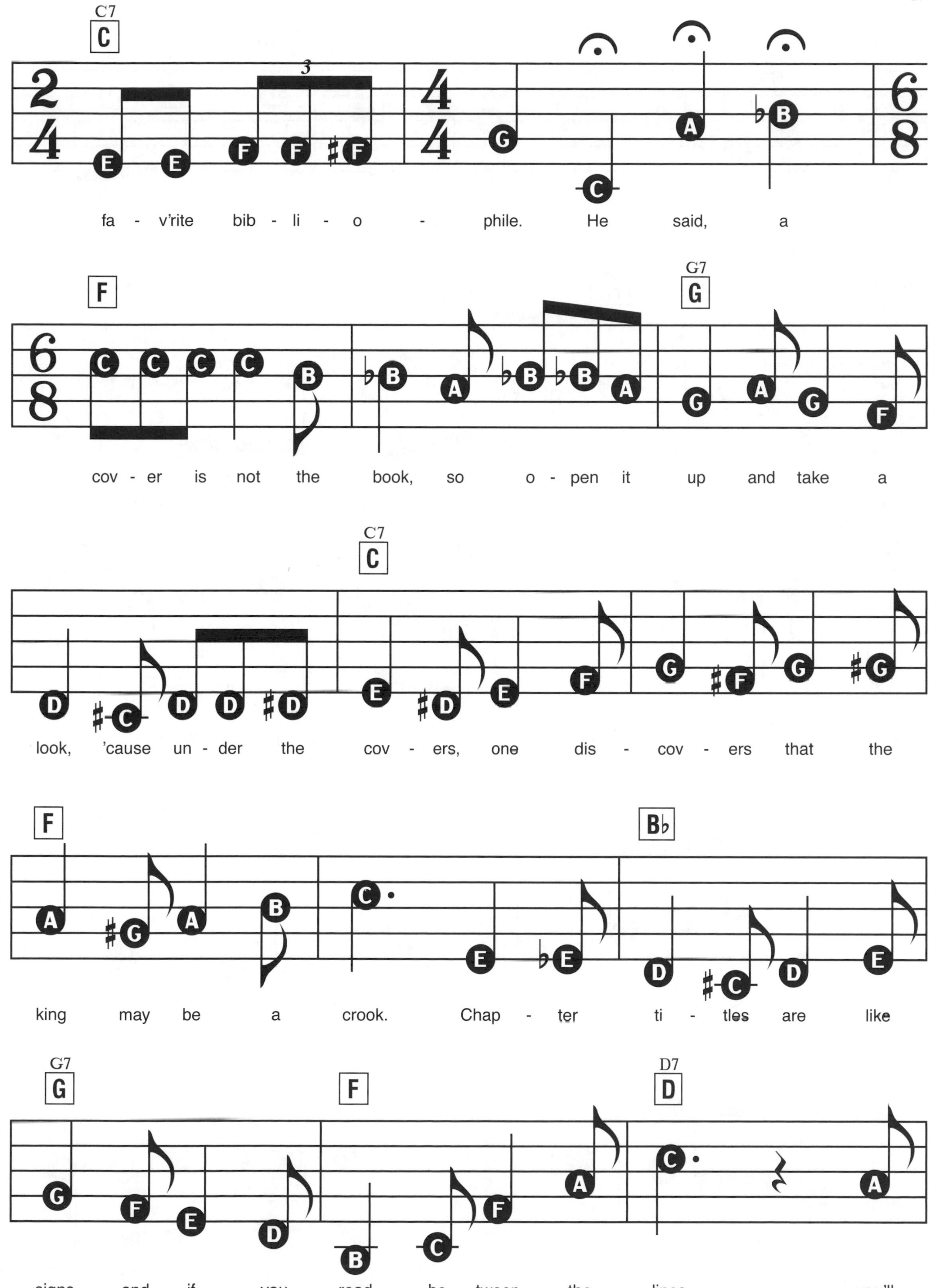
C7
C
3
fa - v'rite bib - li - o - phile. He said, a
F
G7
G
cov - er is not the book, so o - pen it up and take a
C7
C
look, 'cause un - der the cov - ers, one dis - cov - ers that the
F
B♭
king may be a crook. Chap - ter ti - tles are like
G7
G
F
D7
D
signs, and if you read be - tween the lines, you'll

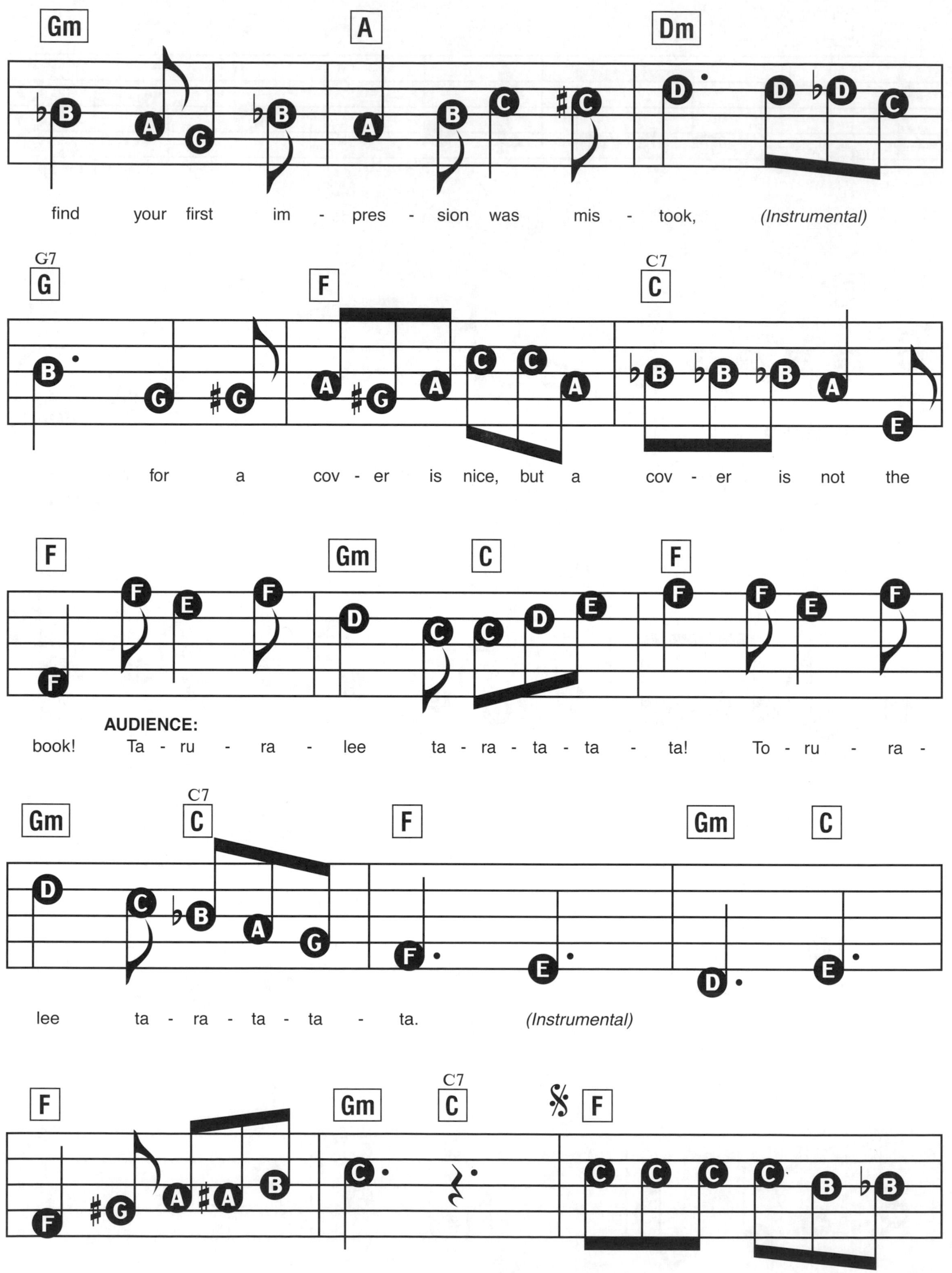
Gm
A
Dm
find your first im - pres - sion was mis - took,
(Instrumental)
G7
G
F
C7
C
for a cov - er is nice, but a cov - er is not the
F
Gm
C
F
AUDIENCE:
book! Ta - ru - ra - lee ta - ra - ta - ta - ta! To - ru - ra -
Gm
C7
C
F
Gm
C
lee ta - ra - ta - ta - ta.
(Instrumental)
F
Gm
C7
C
F
MARY: "Nel - lie Ru - bi - na" was
Hy - a - cinth Ma -

D7
D
G7
G
B
A
G
A
G
A
G
F
D
C
D
D
made of wood, but what could not be seen was though her
caw brought all her treas - ures to a reef, MARY: where she
C7
C
F
E
D
E
F
G
B
C
C
D
F
D
D
trunk up top was bar - ren, well, her roots were lush and
on - ly wore a smi - le, JACK: plus two feath - ers and a
B♭
G7
G
C
C
C
D
C
D
E
G
F
E
D
green. So in spring, when Mis - ter Hick - 'ry saw her
leaf. So no one tried to rob her, 'cause she
F
D
G
B
C
F
A
B
blos - soms bloom - ing there, he took root de - spite her
bare - ly wore a stitch, for when in your birth - day
C7
C
G
C7
C
To Coda
F
A
bark and now there's seed - lings ev - 'ry - where! MARY & JACK: Which
suit, BOTH: there ain't much there to show you're

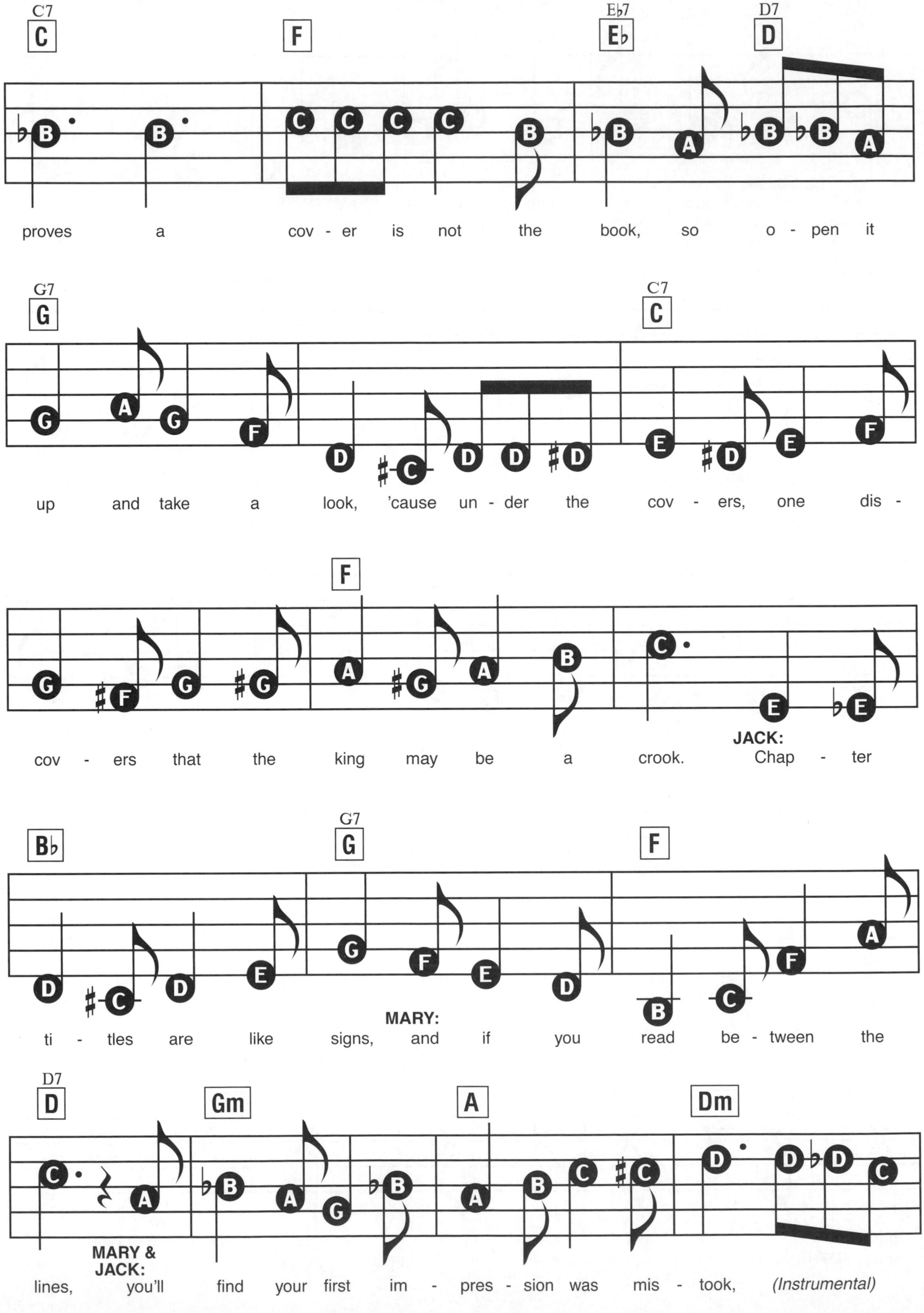

C7 C | F | E♭7 E♭ | D7 D

proves a cov - er is not the book, so o - pen it

G7 G | C7 C

up and take a look, 'cause un - der the cov - ers, one dis -

F

cov - ers that the king may be a crook. **JACK:** Chap - ter

B♭ | G7 G | F

ti - tles are like signs, **MARY:** and if you read be - tween the

D7 D | Gm | A | Dm

lines, **MARY & JACK:** you'll find your first im - pres - sion was mis - took, *(Instrumental)*

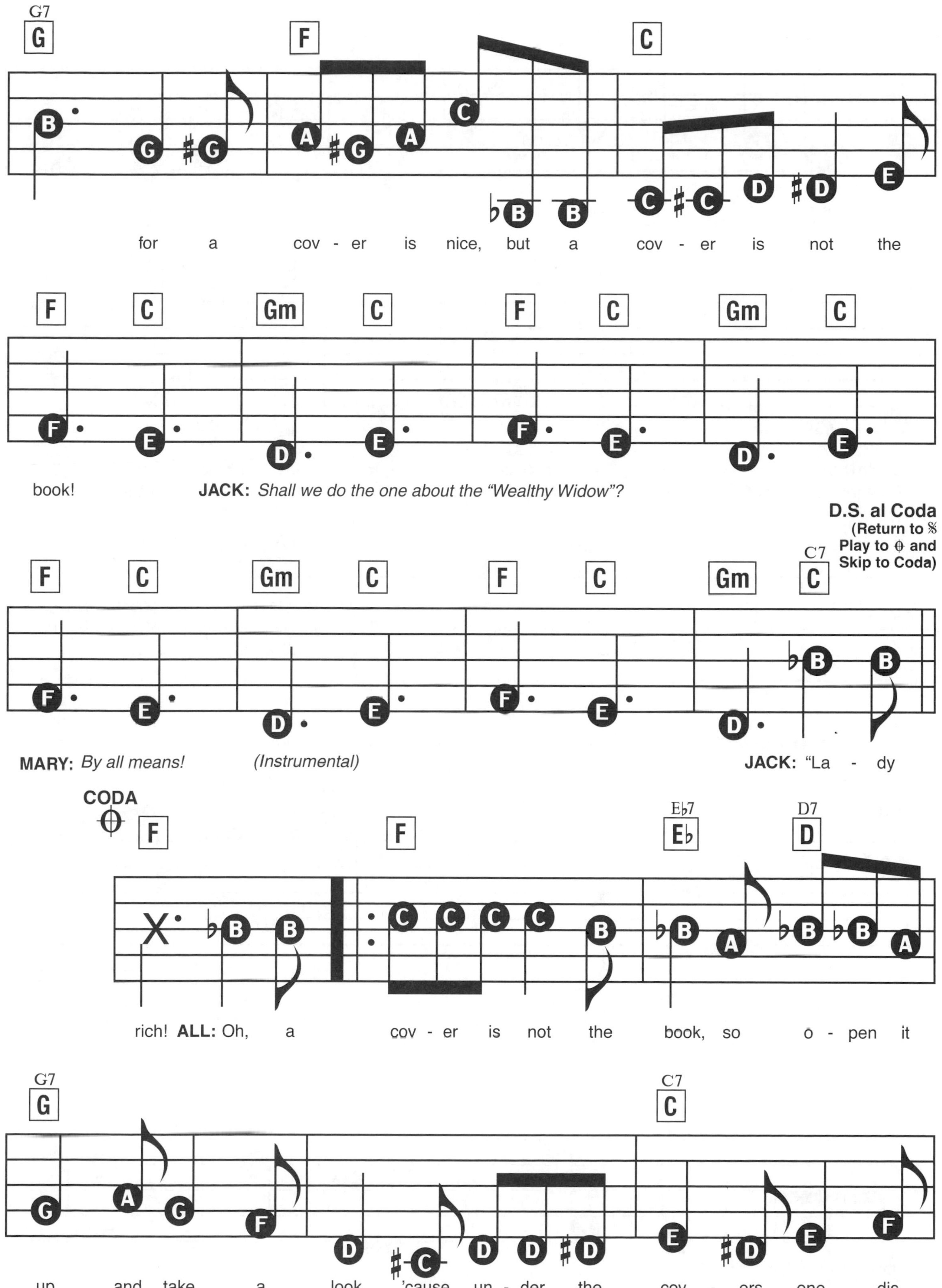
G7
G
F
C
for a cov - er is nice, but a cov - er is not the
F C Gm C F C Gm C
book! JACK: Shall we do the one about the "Wealthy Widow"?
D.S. al Coda
(Return to 𝄋
Play to ⊕ and
Skip to Coda)
F C Gm C F C Gm C7 C
MARY: By all means! (Instrumental) JACK: "La - dy
CODA
F F E♭7 E♭ D7 D
rich! ALL: Oh, a cov - er is not the book, so o - pen it
G7 G C7 C
up and take a look, 'cause un - der the cov - ers one dis -

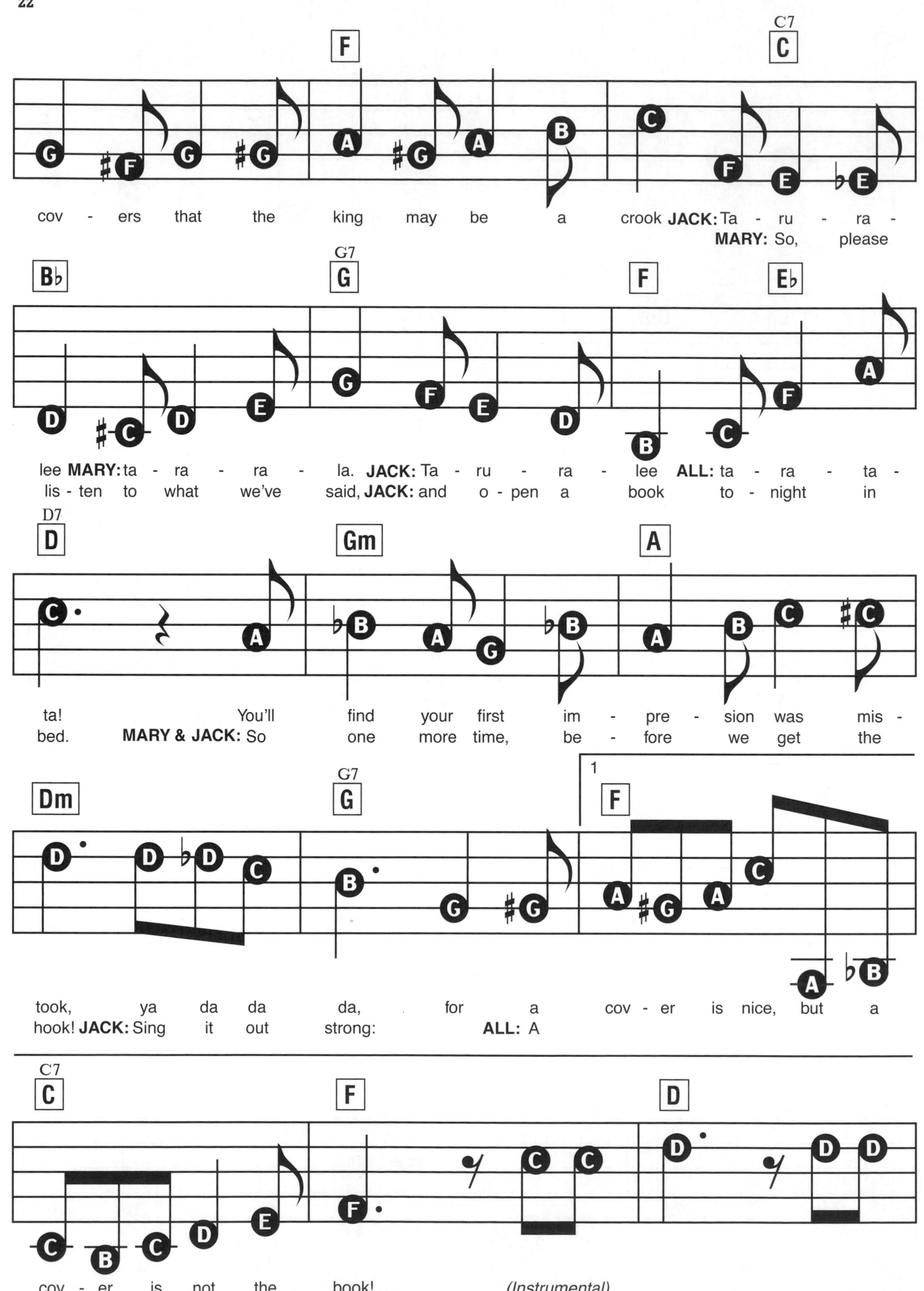
F C7 C
cov - ers that the king may be a crook JACK: Ta - ru - ra -
MARY: So, please
B♭ G7 G F E♭
lee MARY: ta - ra - ra - la. JACK: Ta - ru - ra - lee ALL: ta - ra - ta -
lis - ten to what we've said, JACK: and o - pen a book to - night in
D7 D Gm A
ta! You'll find your first im - pre - sion was mis -
bed. MARY & JACK: So one more time, be - fore we get the
Dm G7 G 1 F
took, ya da da da, for a cov - er is nice, but a
hook! JACK: Sing it out strong: ALL: A
C7 C F D
cov - er is not the book! (Instrumental)

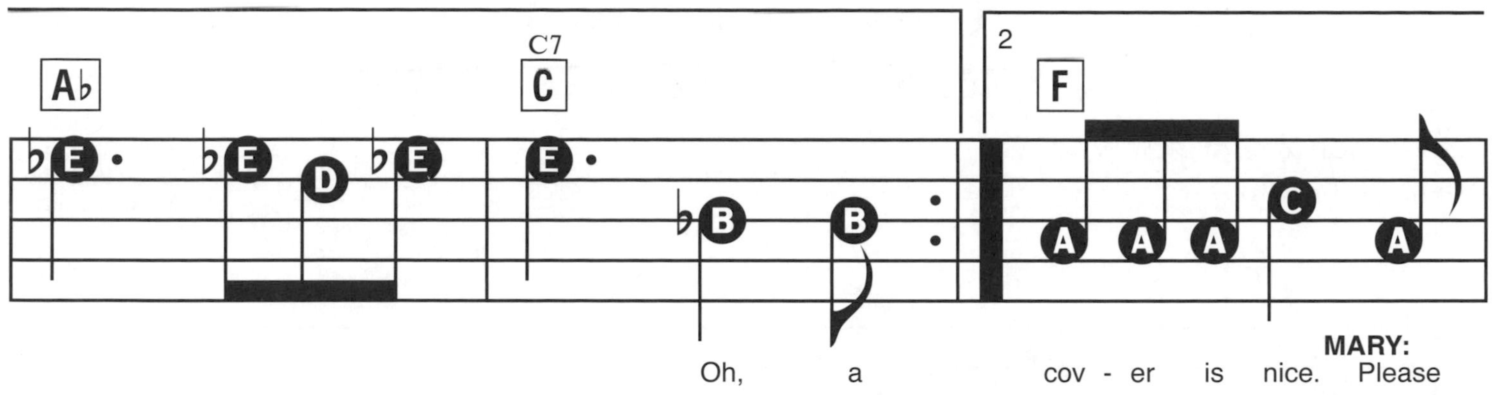
C7
2
MARY:
Oh, a cov - er is nice. Please

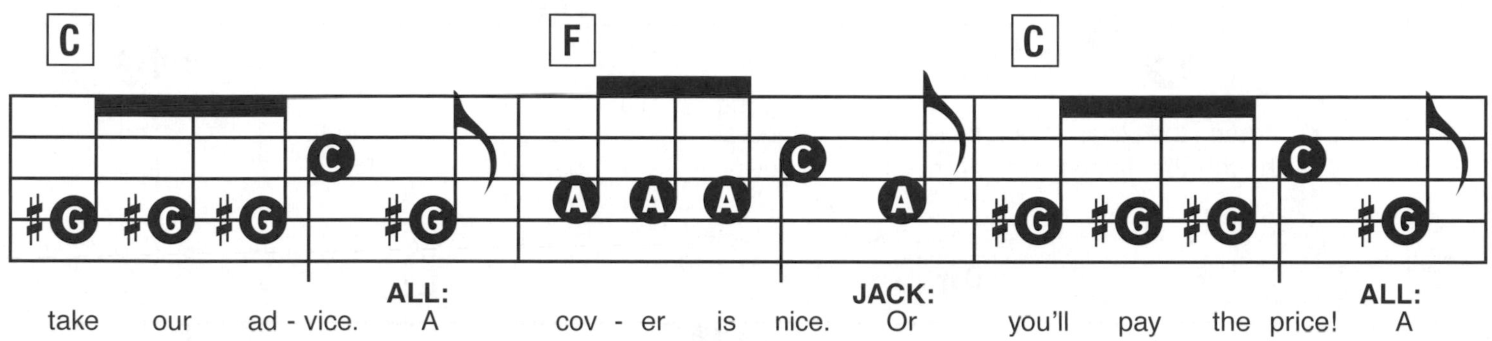
ALL:
JACK:
ALL:
take our ad - vice. A cov - er is nice. Or you'll pay the price! A

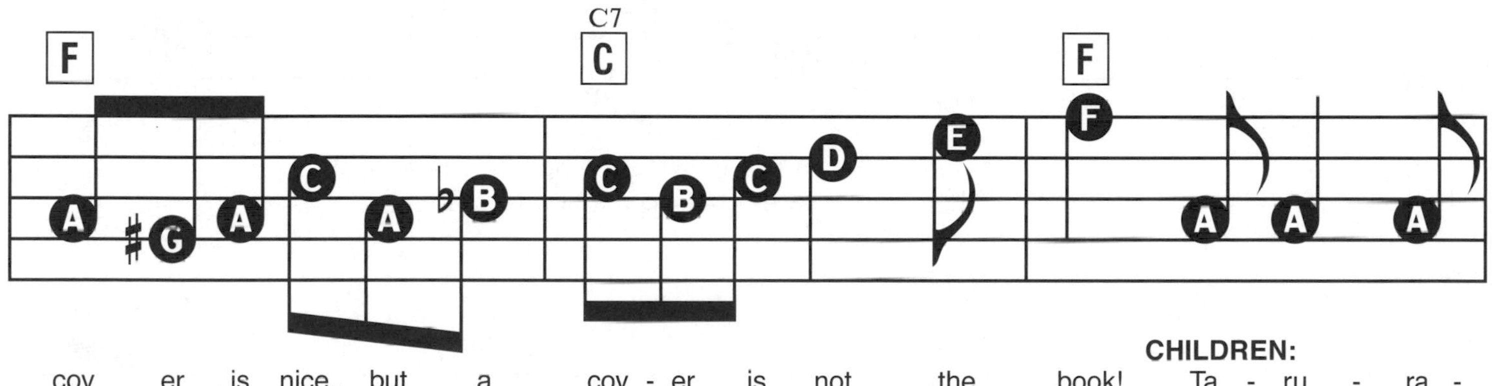
C7
CHILDREN:
cov er is nice., but a cov - er is not the book! Ta - ru - ra -

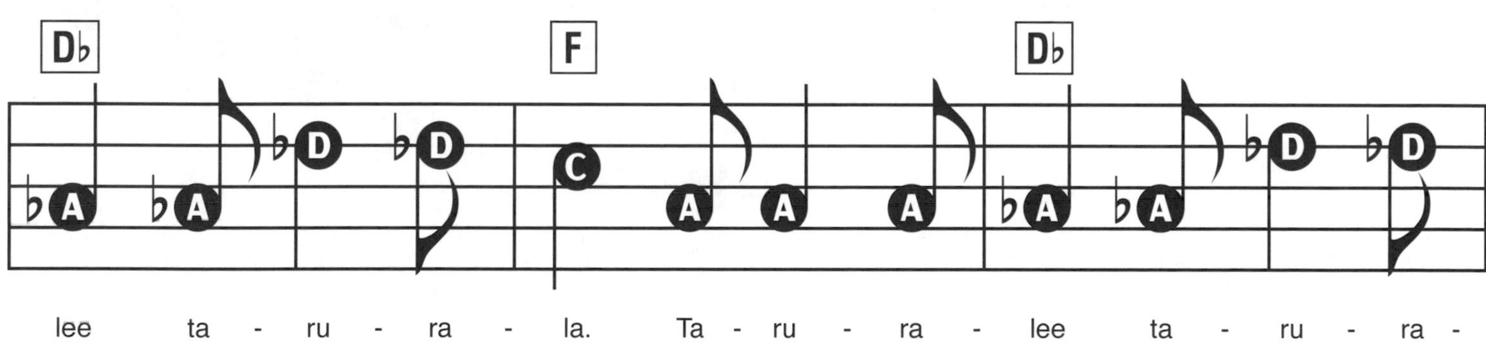
lee ta - ru - ra - la. Ta - ru - ra - lee ta - ru - ra -

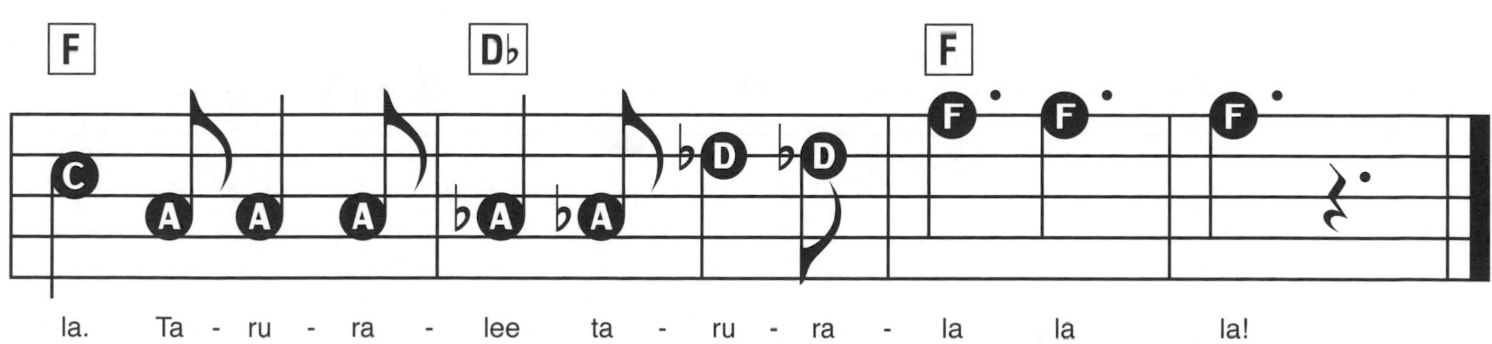
la. Ta - ru - ra - lee ta - ru - ra - la la la!

(Underneath the)
Lovely London Sky

Registration 2
Rhythm: Waltz

Music by Marc Shaiman
Lyrics by Scott Wittman
and Marc Shaiman

C Dm

JACK: When the ear - ly morn - ing hours have come and
Though the lamps I'm turn - ing down, please don't feel

G7 Dm G7

gone, through the mist - y morn - ing showers I
blue. In this part of Lon - don town, the

C G7 C

greet the dawn. For when its light has hit the
light shines through. Don't be - lieve the things you've

E7 F Fm

ground, there's lots of trea - sures to be found,
read; you nev - er know what's up a - head

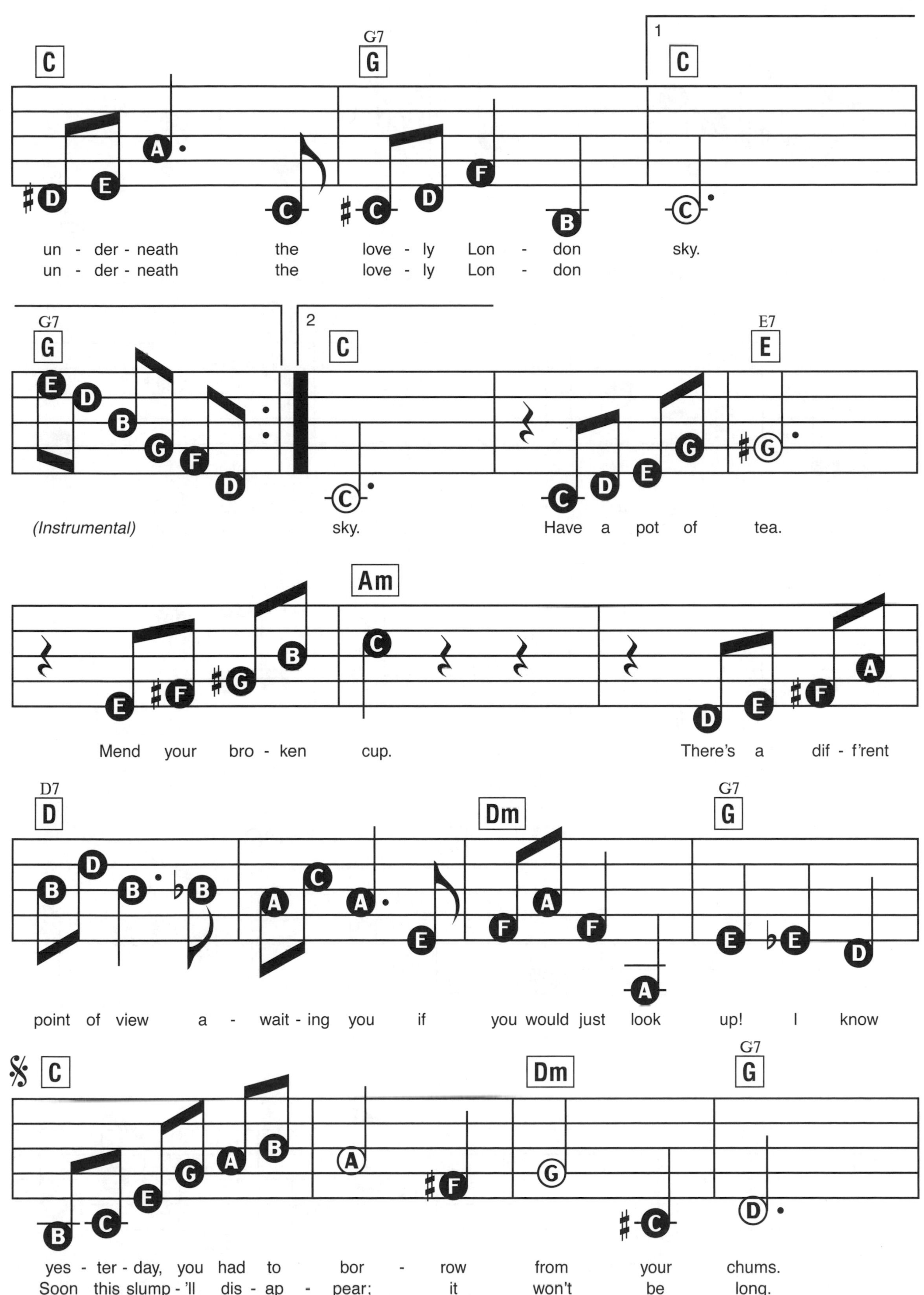
C G7 G 1 C
un - der - neath the love - ly Lon - don sky.
un - der - neath the love - ly Lon - don
G7 G 2 C E7 E
(Instrumental) sky. Have a pot of tea.
Am
Mend your bro - ken cup. There's a dif - f'rent
D7 D Dm G7 G
point of view a - wait - ing you if you would just look up! I know
C Dm G7 G
yes - ter - day, you had to bor - row from your chums.
Soon this slump - 'll dis - ap - pear; it won't be long.

Dm
G7
G
C
Seems the prom - ise of to - mor - row nev - er comes. But,
Soon - er than ya think, you'll hear some bright new song. So,
E7
E
F
since you dreamed the night a - way, to - mor - row's here! It's
hold on tight to those you love, and may - be soon, from
Fm
C
E7
E
called to - day! So, count your bless - ings, you're a luck - y
up a - bove, you'll be blessed. So keep on look - ing
Am
D
C
To Coda
G7
G
guy. For you're un - der - neath the love - ly Lon - don
high, while you're un - der - neath the
C
E7
E
sky. (Instrumental)

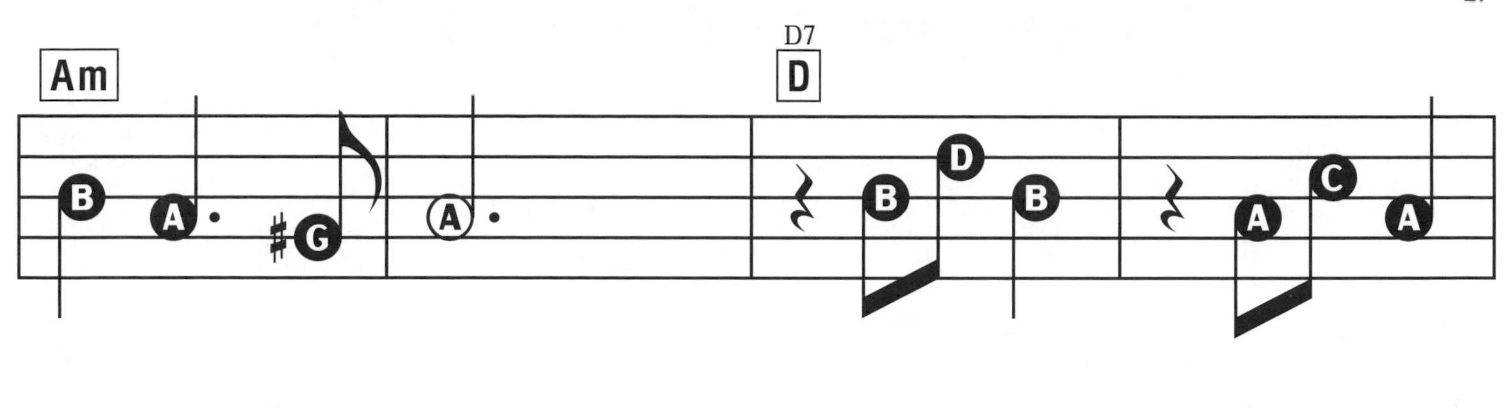
Am
D7
D
B
A
G
A
B
D
B
A
C
A

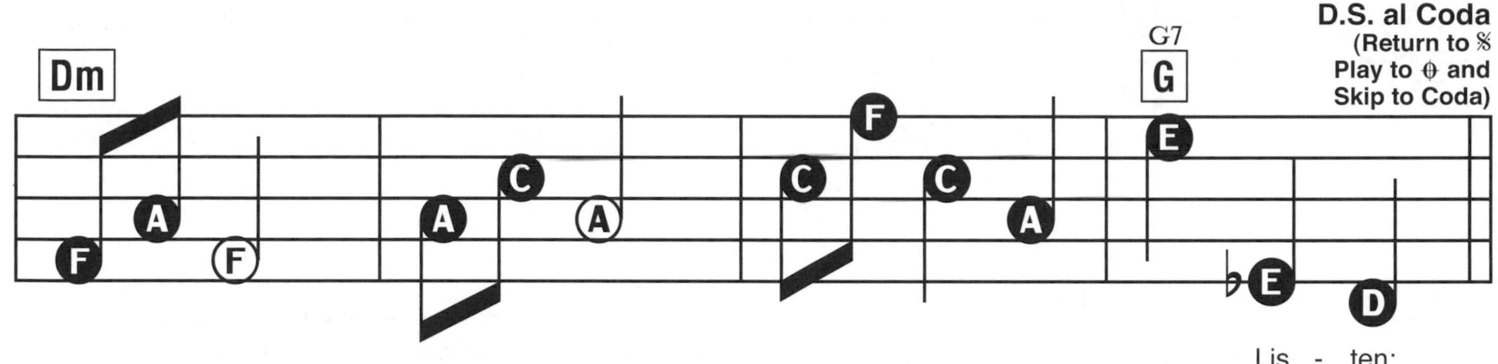
Dm
G7
G
D.S. al Coda
(Return to 𝄋
Play to ⊕ and
Skip to Coda)
F
A
F
A
C
A
C
F
C
A
E
E
D
Lis - ten:

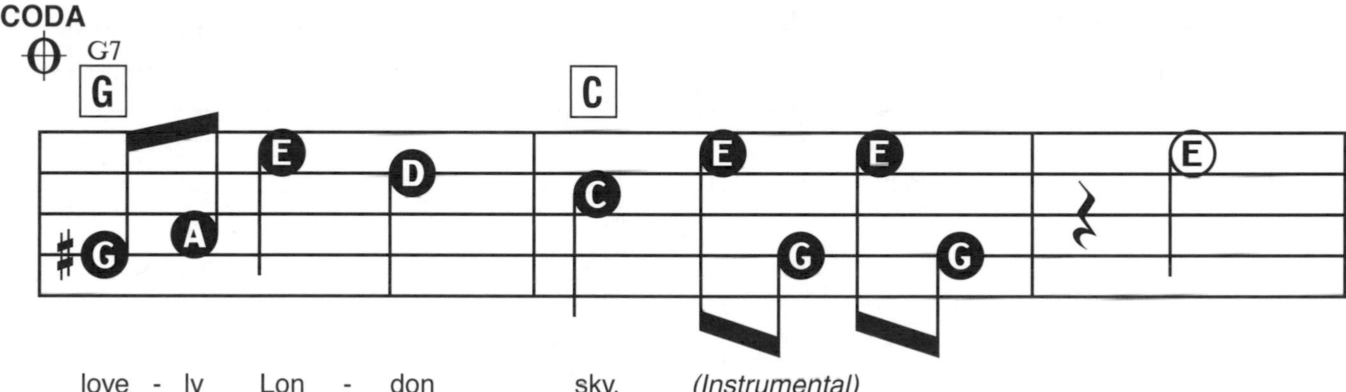
CODA
G7
G
C
G
A
E
D
C
E
G
E
G
E
love - ly Lon - don sky. (Instrumental)

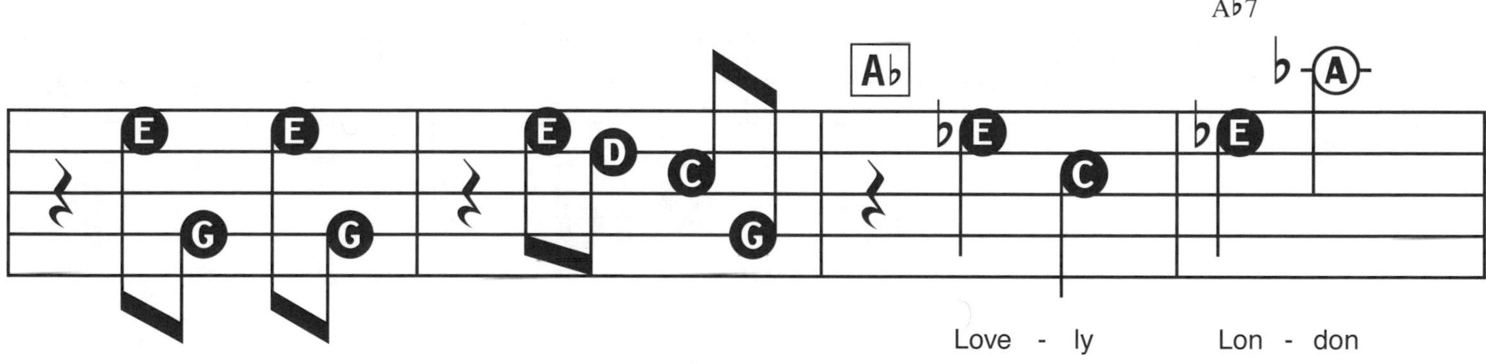
A♭7
A♭
E
G
E
G
E
D
C
G
E
C
E
A
Love - ly Lon - don

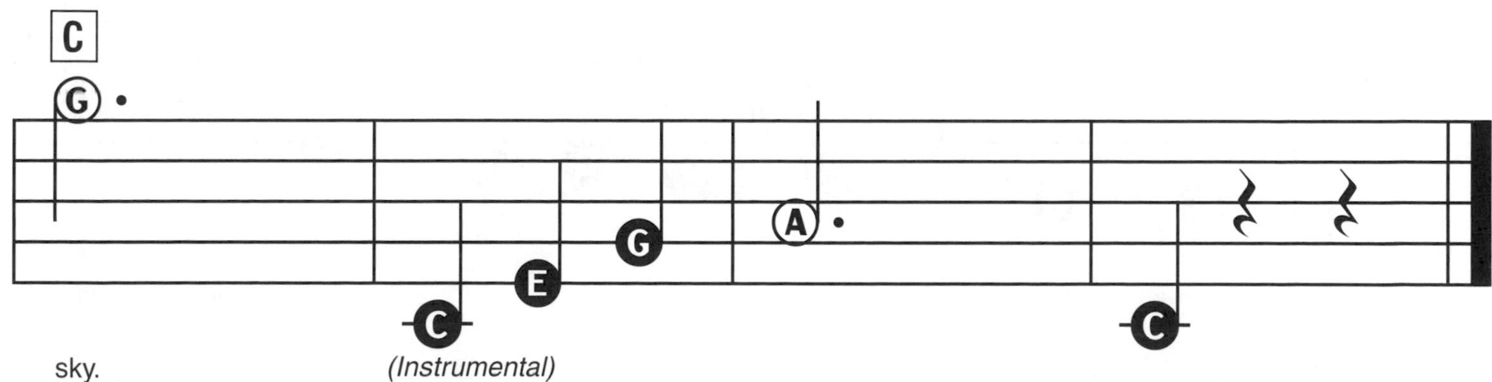
C
G
C
E
G
A
C
sky.
(Instrumental)

Nowhere to Go But Up

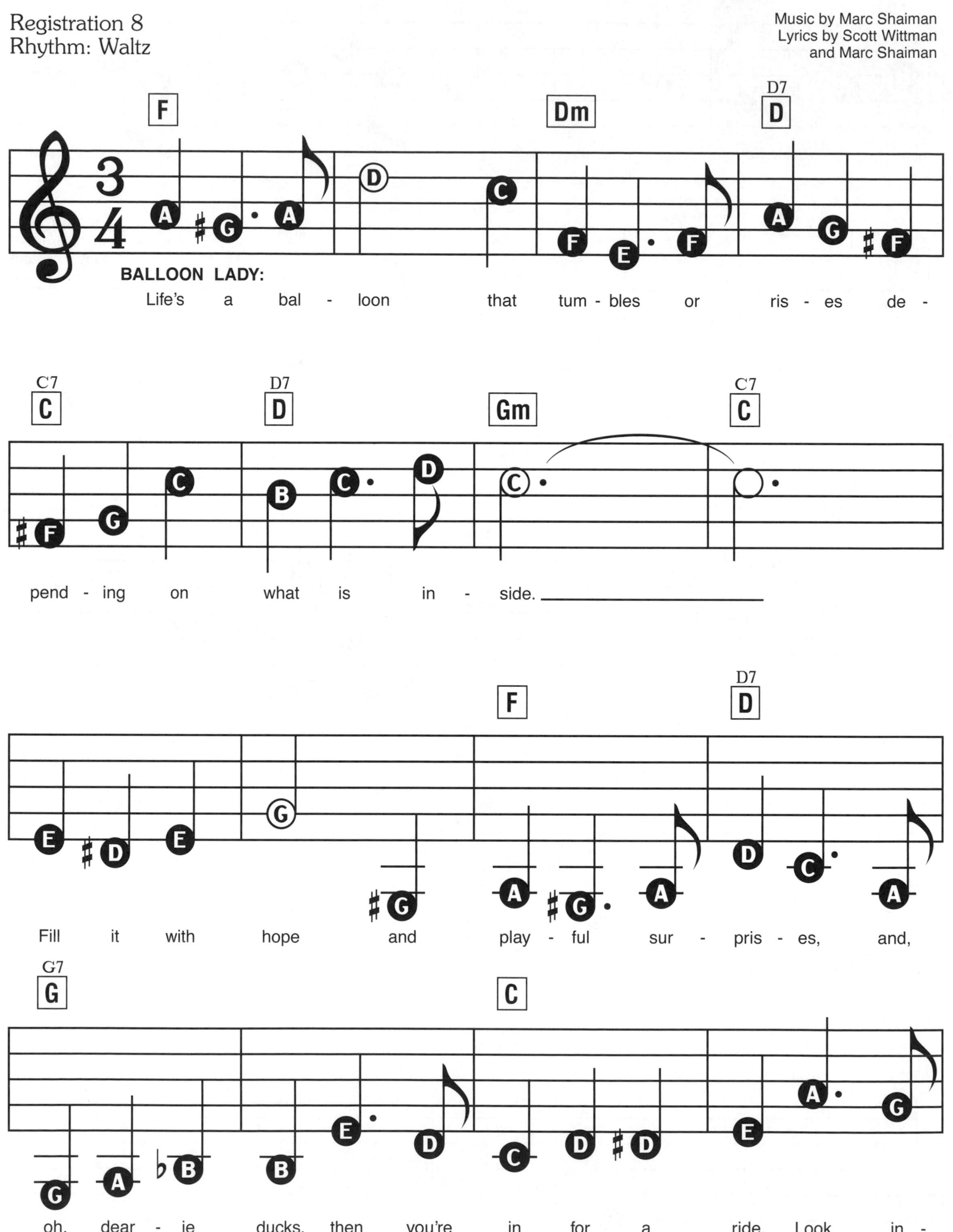
Registration 8
Rhythm: Waltz
Music by Marc Shaiman
Lyrics by Scott Wittman
and Marc Shaiman
F
Dm
D7
D
A
G
A
D
C
F
E
F
A
G
F
BALLOON LADY:
Life's a bal - loon that tum - bles or ris - es de -
C7
C
D7
D
Gm
C7
C
F
G
C
B
C
D
C
pend - ing on what is in - side.
F
D7
D
E
D
E
G
G
A
G
A
D
C
A
Fill it with hope and play - ful sur - pris - es, and,
G7
G
C
G
A
B
B
E
D
C
D
D
E
A
G
oh, dear - ie ducks, then you're in for a ride. Look in -

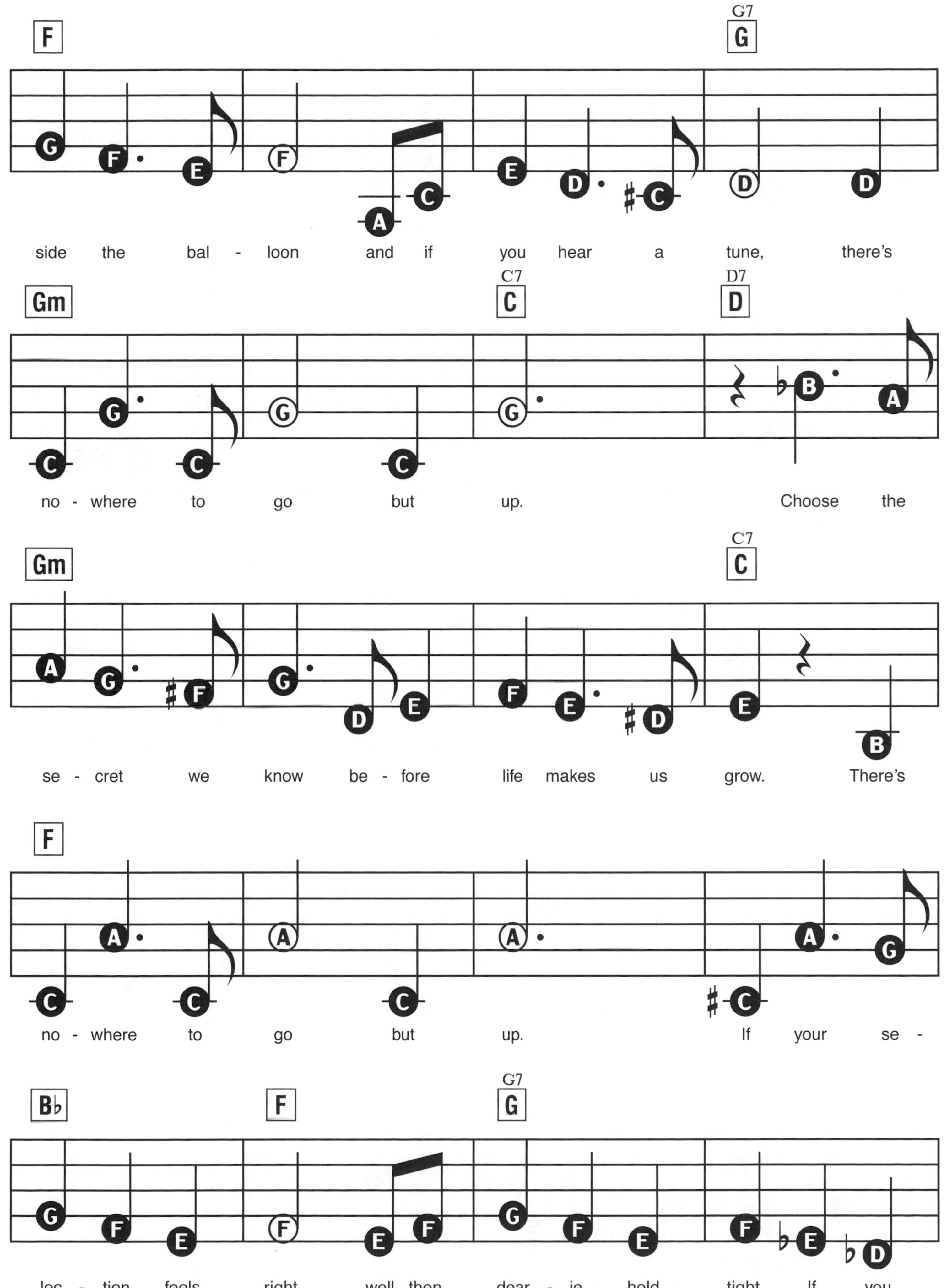
F
G7
G
side the bal - loon and if you hear a tune, there's
Gm
C7
C
D7
D
no - where to go but up. Choose the
Gm
C7
C
se - cret we know be - fore life makes us grow. There's
F
no - where to go but up. If your se -
B♭
F
G7
G
lec - tion feels right, well then, dear - ie, hold tight. If you

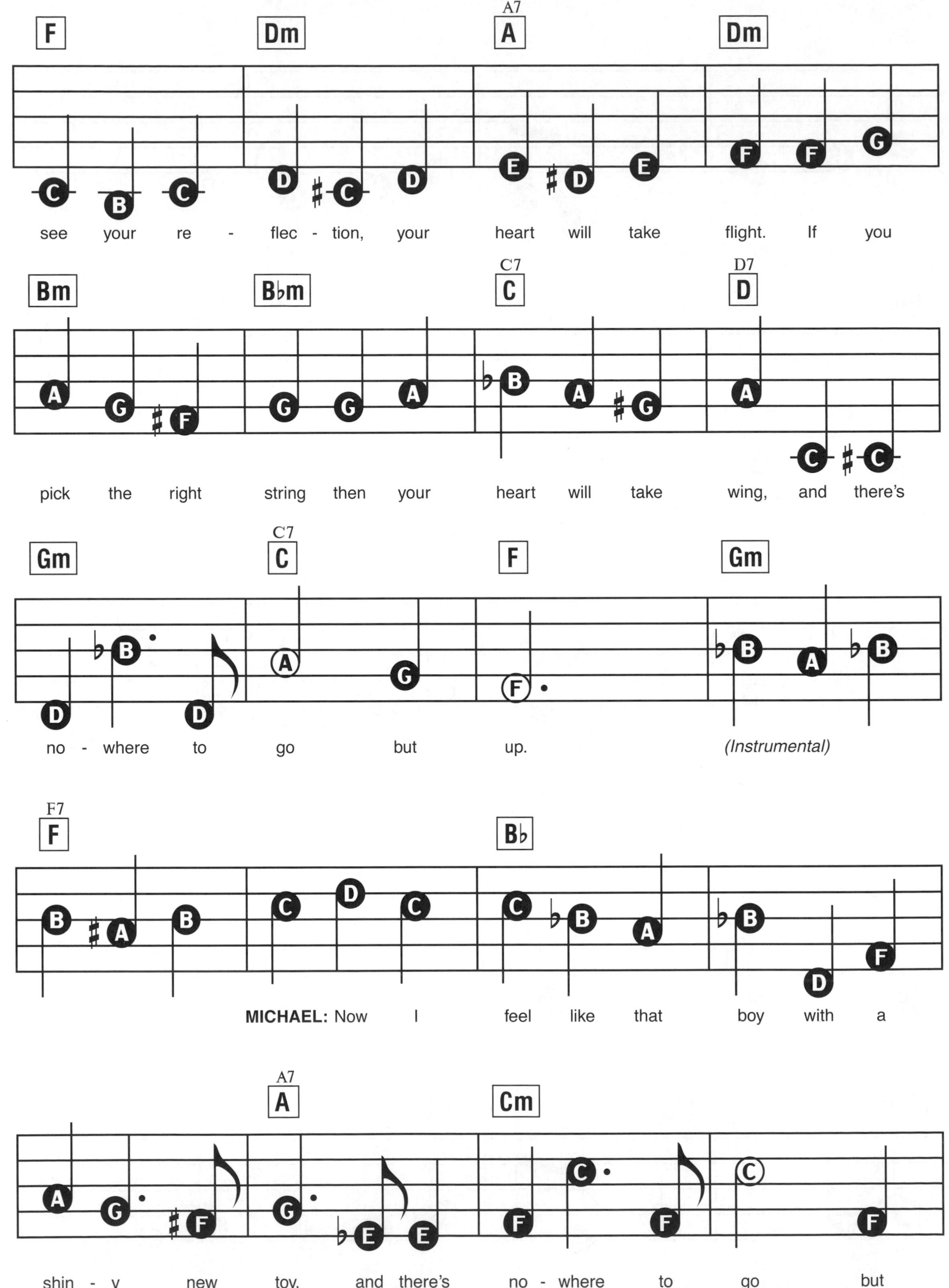
F Dm A7 A Dm
see your re - flec - tion, your heart will take flight. If you
Bm B♭m C7 C D7 D
pick the right string then your heart will take wing, and there's
Gm C7 C F Gm
no - where to go but up.
(Instrumental)
F7 F B♭
MICHAEL: Now I feel like that boy with a
A7 A Cm
shin - y new toy, and there's no - where to go but

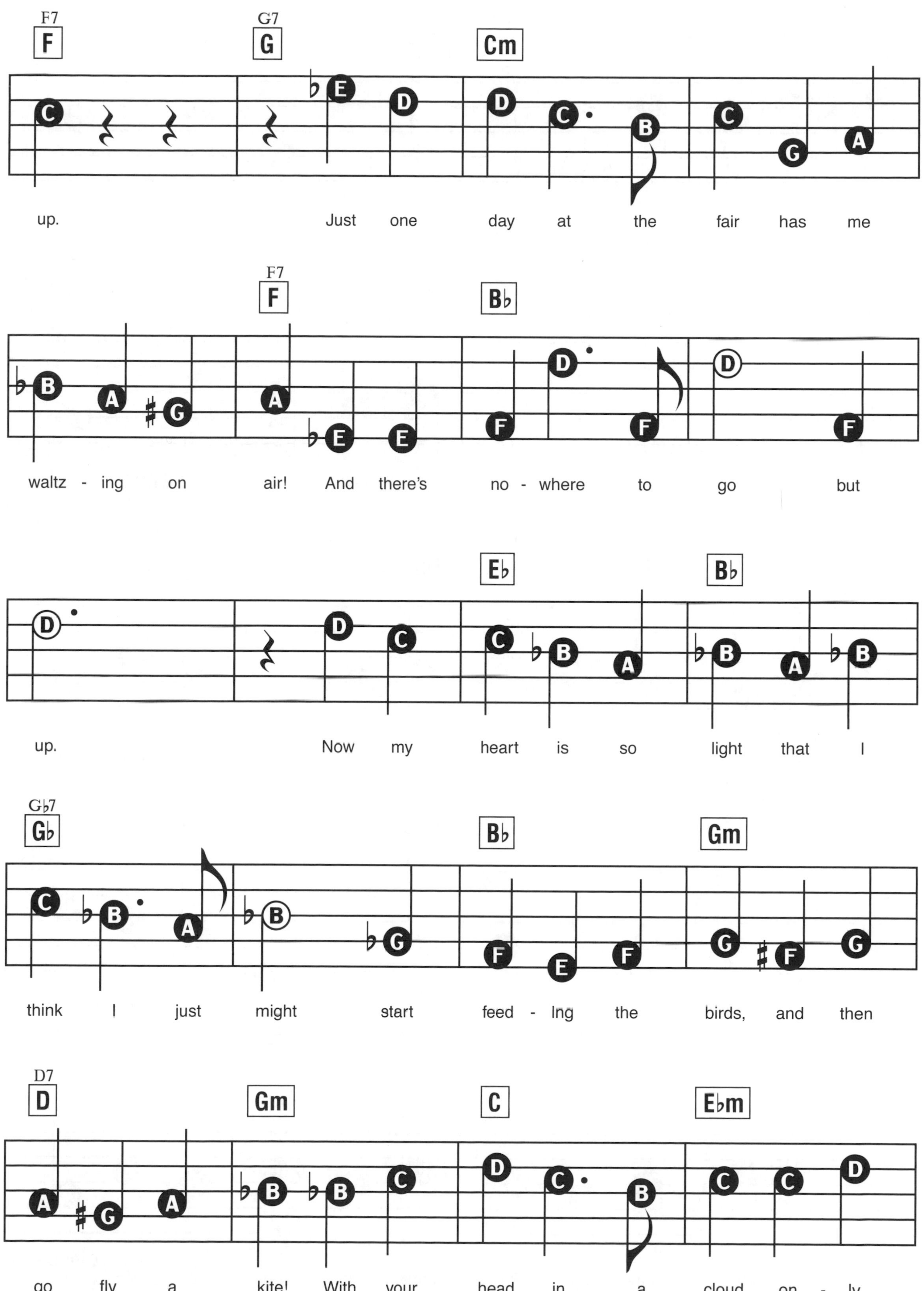
F7 F G7 G Cm
up. Just one day at the fair has me
F7 F B♭
waltz - ing on air! And there's no - where to go but
E♭ B♭
up. Now my heart is so light that I
G♭7 G♭ B♭ Gm
think I just might start feed - ing the birds, and then
D7 D Gm C E♭m
go fly a kite! With your head in a cloud on - ly

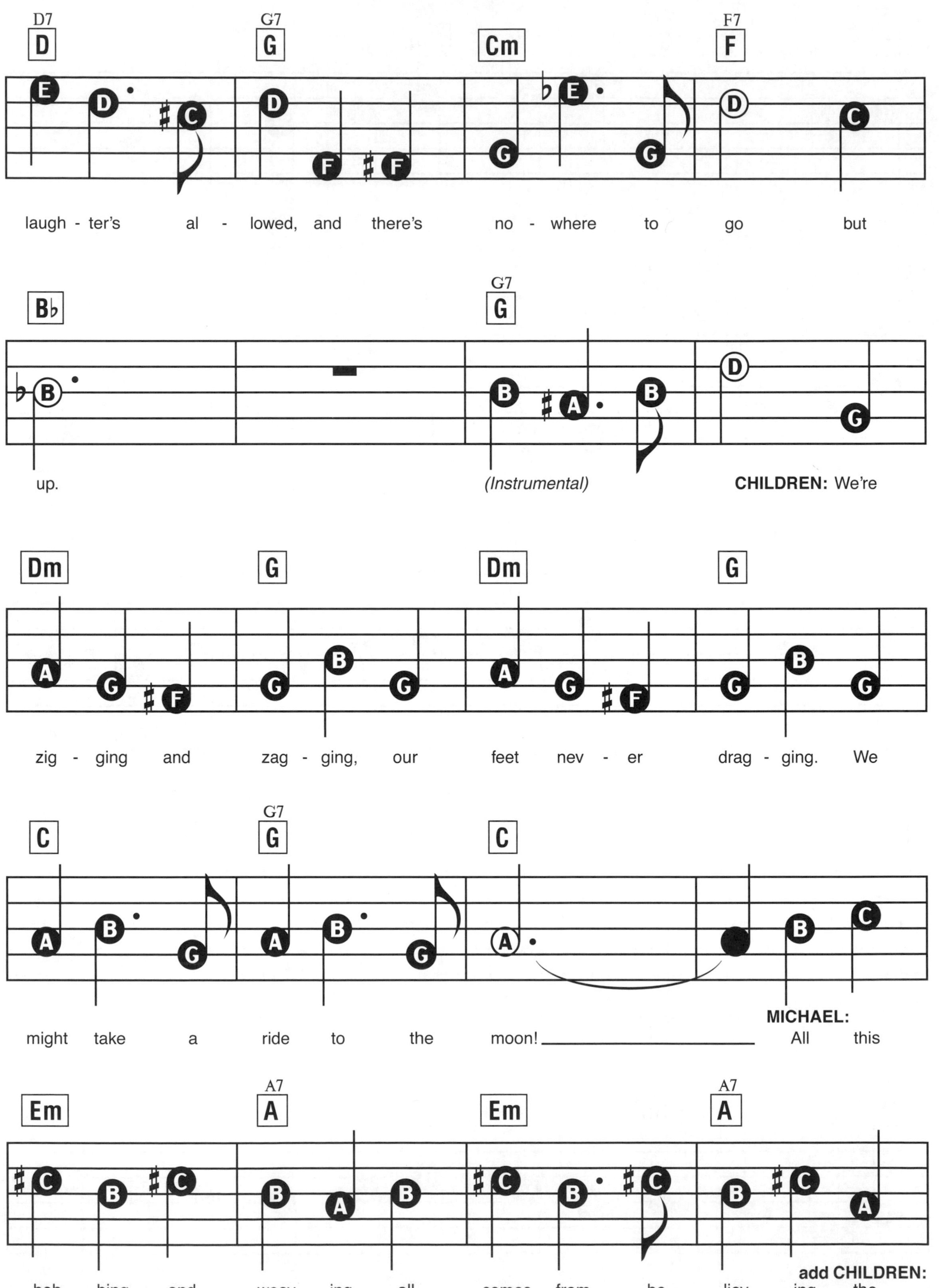
D7
D
G7
G
Cm
F7
F
laugh - ter's al - lowed, and there's no - where to go but
B♭
G7
G
up.
(Instrumental)
CHILDREN: We're
Dm
G
Dm
G
zig - ging and zag - ging, our feet nev - er drag - ging. We
C
G7
G
C
might take a ride to the moon!
MICHAEL:
All this
Em
A7
A
Em
A7
A
bob - bing and weav - ing all comes from be - liev - ing the
add CHILDREN:

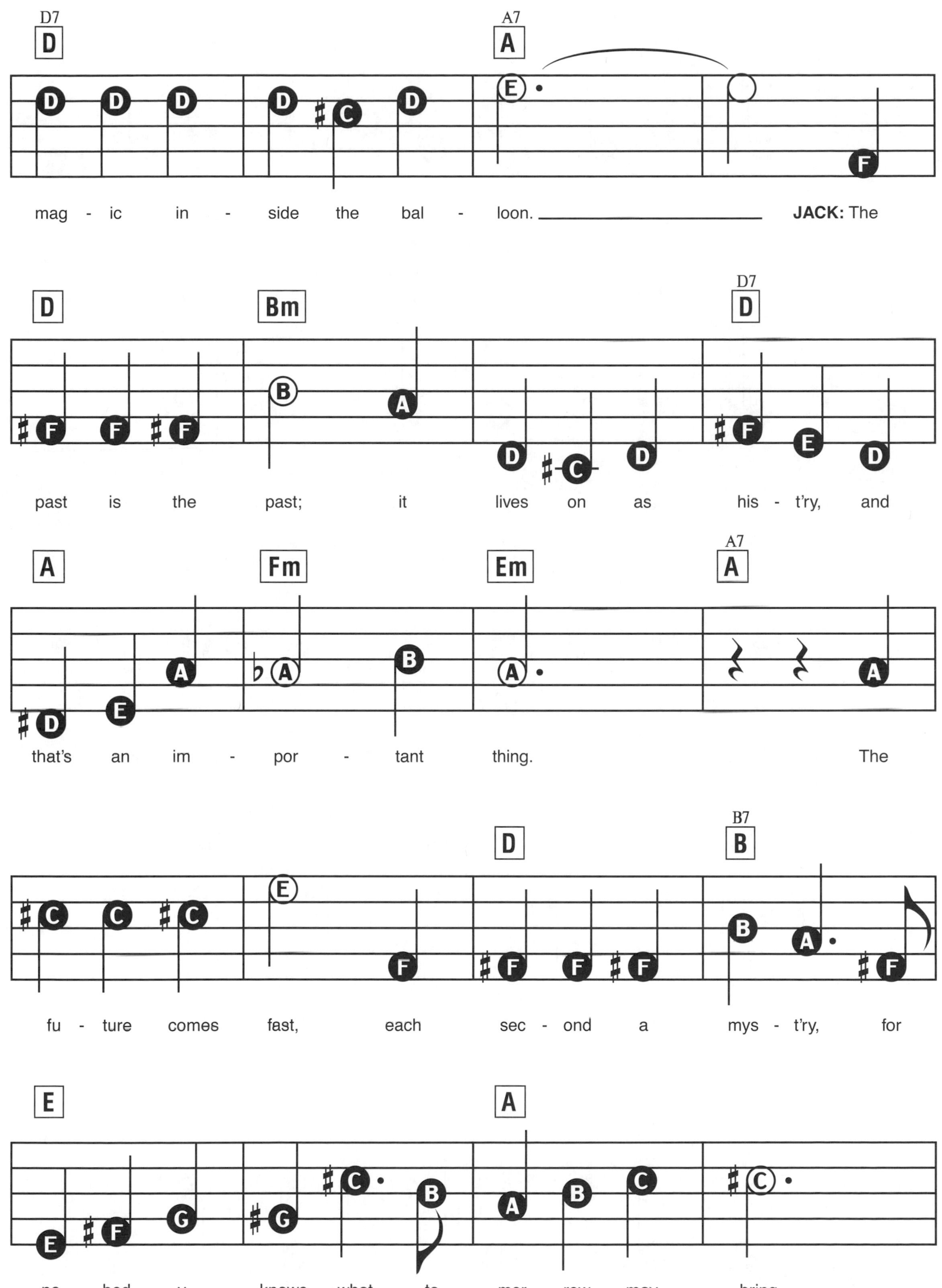
D7
D
A7
A
D D D D C D E F
mag - ic in - side the bal - loon.
JACK: The
D
Bm
D7
D
F F F B A D C D F E D
past is the past; it lives on as his - t'ry, and
A
Fm
Em
A7
A
D E A A B A A
that's an im - por - tant thing.
The
D
B7
B
C C C E F F F F B A F
fu - ture comes fast, each sec - ond a mys - t'ry, for
E
A
E F G G C B A B C C
no - bod - y knows what to - mor - row may bring.

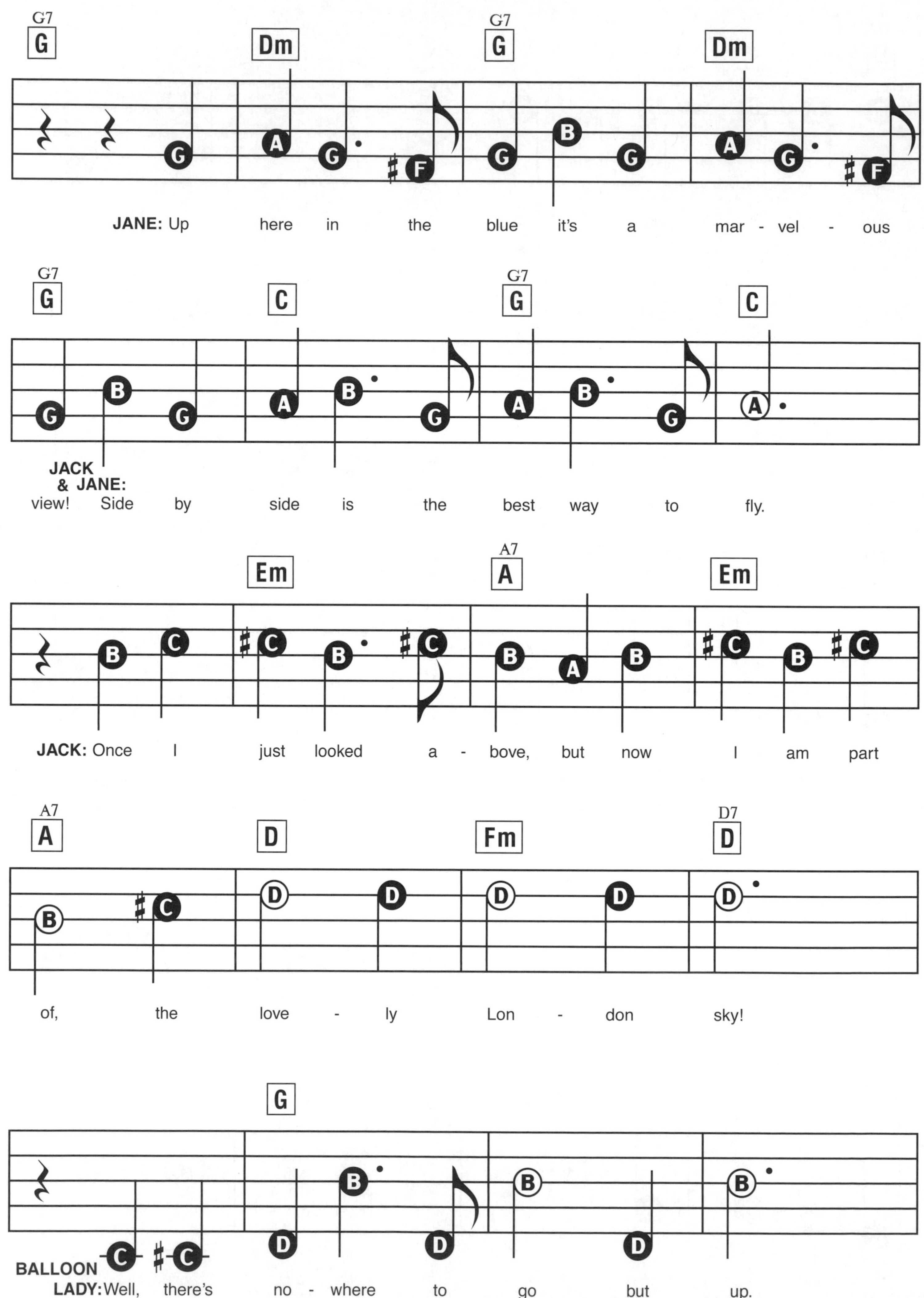
G7 G Dm G7 G Dm
JANE: Up here in the blue it's a mar - vel - ous
G7 G C G7 G C
JACK & JANE:
view! Side by side is the best way to fly.
Em A7 A Em
JACK: Once I just looked a - bove, but now I am part
A7 A D Fm D7 D
of, the love - ly Lon - don sky!
G
BALLOON LADY: Well, there's no - where to go but up.

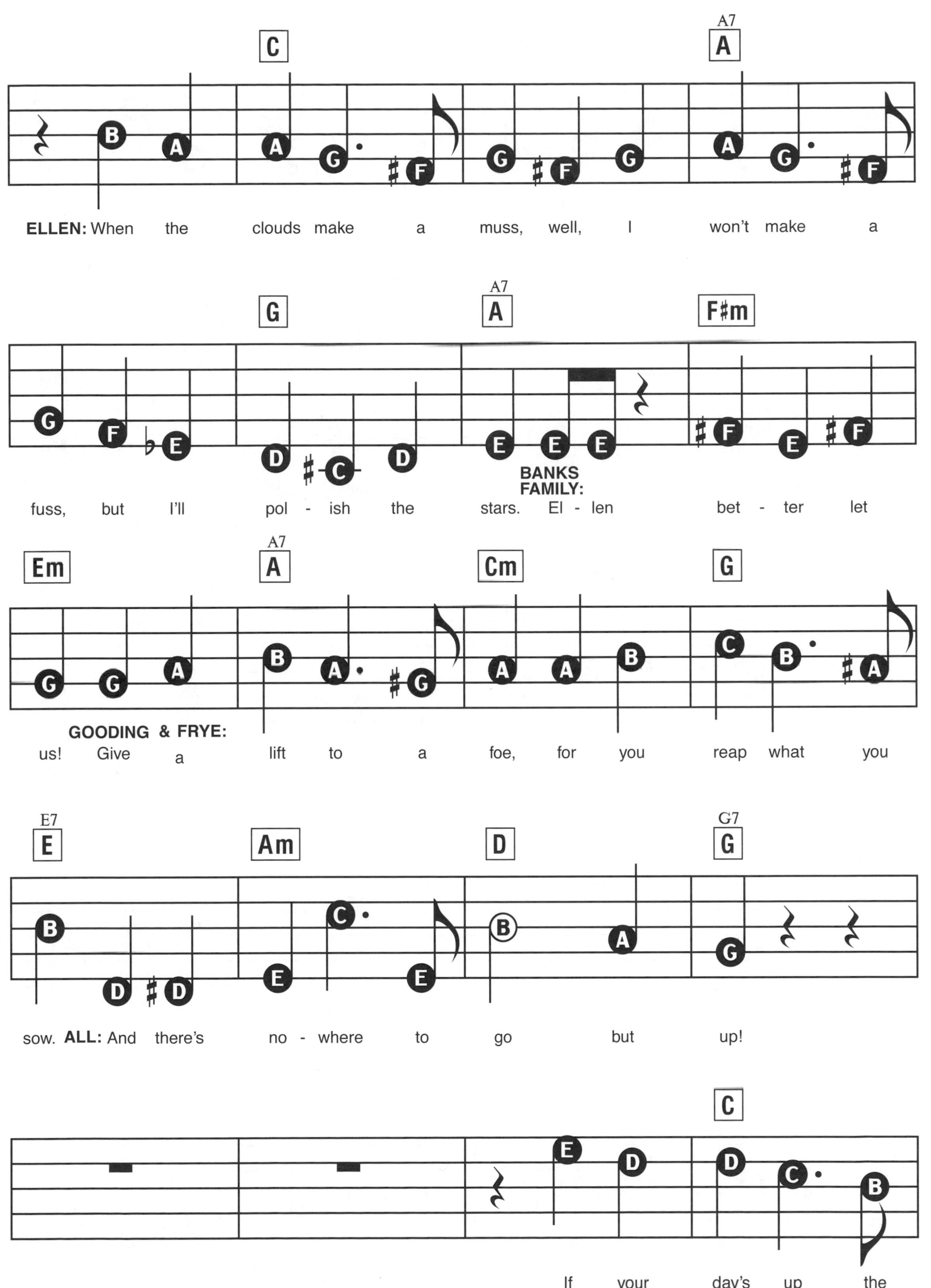
C
A7
A
ELLEN: When the clouds make a muss, well, I won't make a
G
A7
A
F♯m
fuss, but I'll pol - ish the stars.
BANKS FAMILY:
El - len bet - ter let
Em
A7
A
Cm
G
GOODING & FRYE:
us! Give a lift to a foe, for you reap what you
E7
E
Am
D
G7
G
sow. ALL: And there's no - where to go but up!
C
If your day's up the

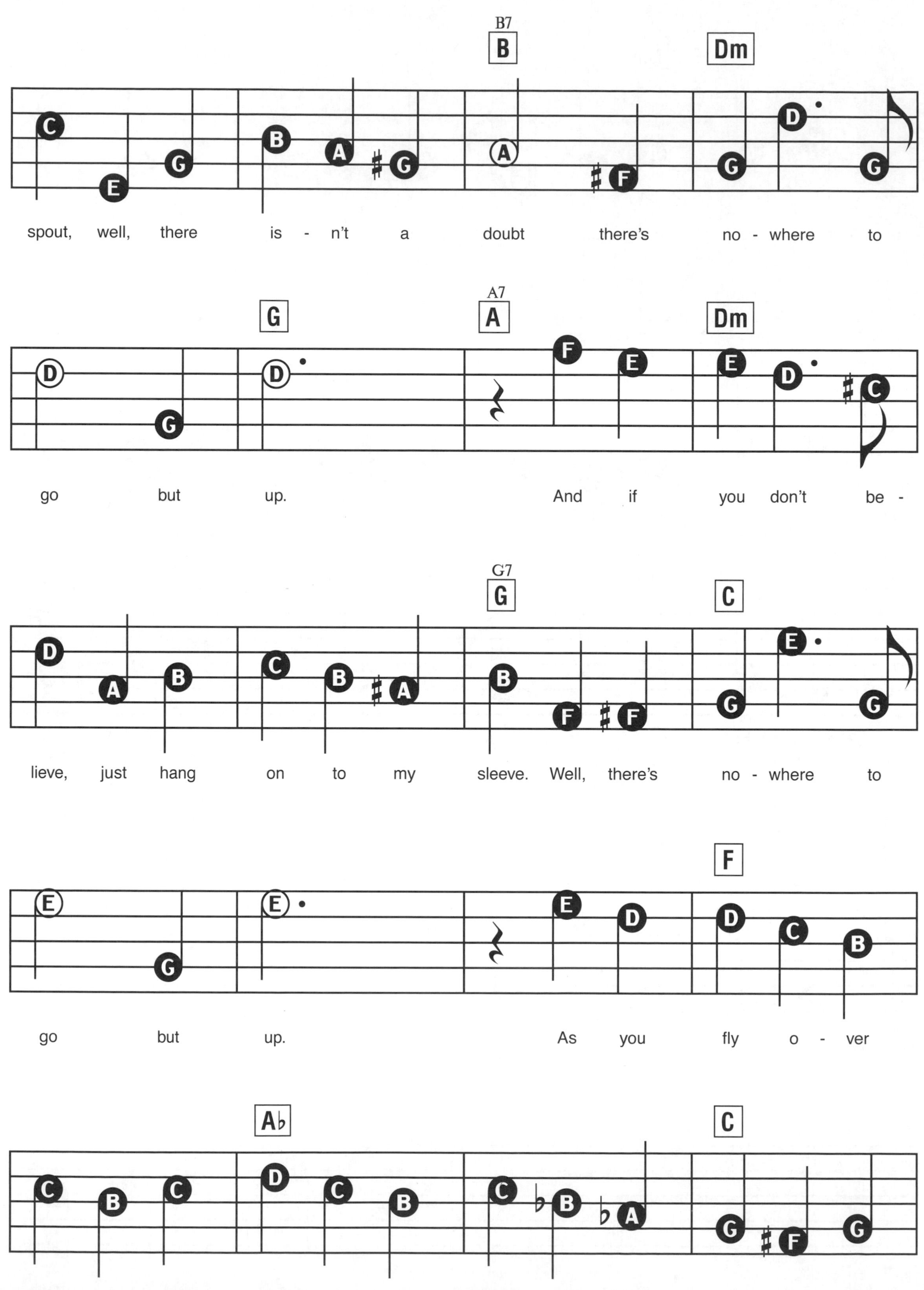
B7 B
Dm
spout, well, there is - n't a doubt there's no - where to
G
A7 A
Dm
go but up. And if you don't be -
G7 G
C
lieve, just hang on to my sleeve. Well, there's no - where to
F
go but up. As you fly o - ver
A♭
C
town it gets hard - er to frown, and we'll all hit the

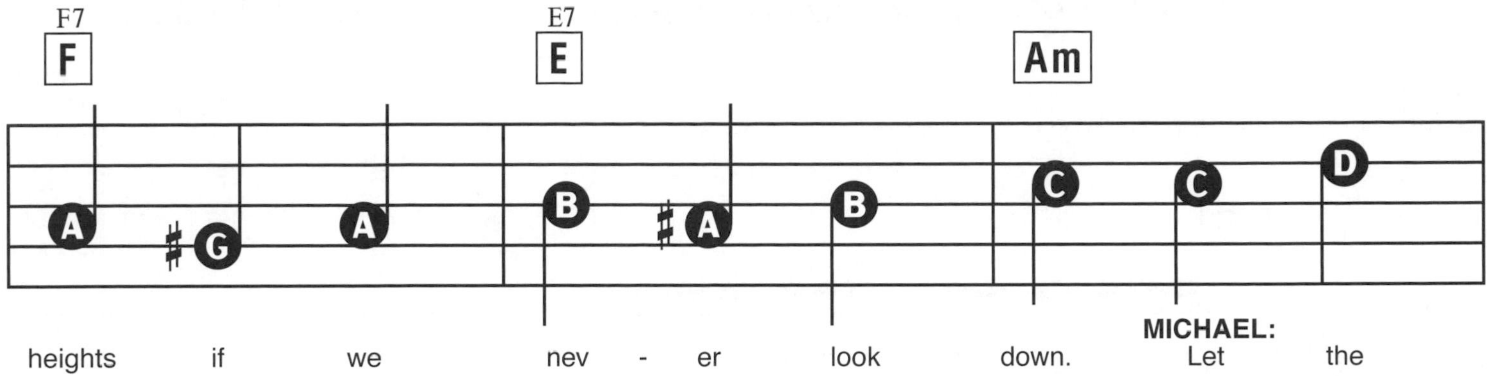
F7
F
E7
E
Am
A
G
A
B
A
B
C
C
D
heights if we nev - er look down. MICHAEL: Let the

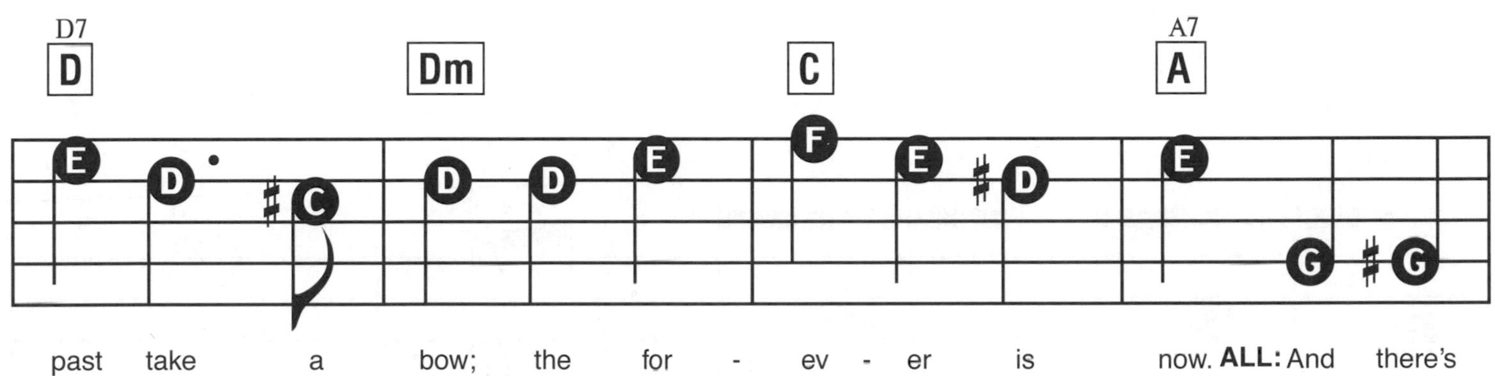
D7
D
Dm
C
A7
A
E
D
C
D
D
E
F
E
D
E
G
G
past take a bow; the for - ev - er is now. ALL: And there's

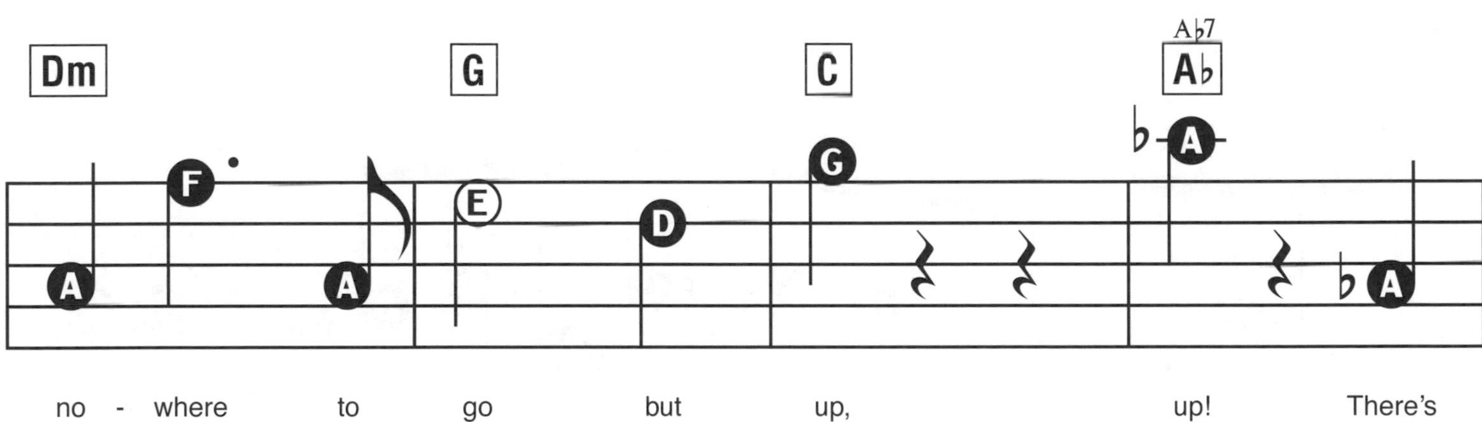
Dm
G
C
A♭7
A♭
A
F
A
E
D
G
A
A
no - where to go but up, up! There's

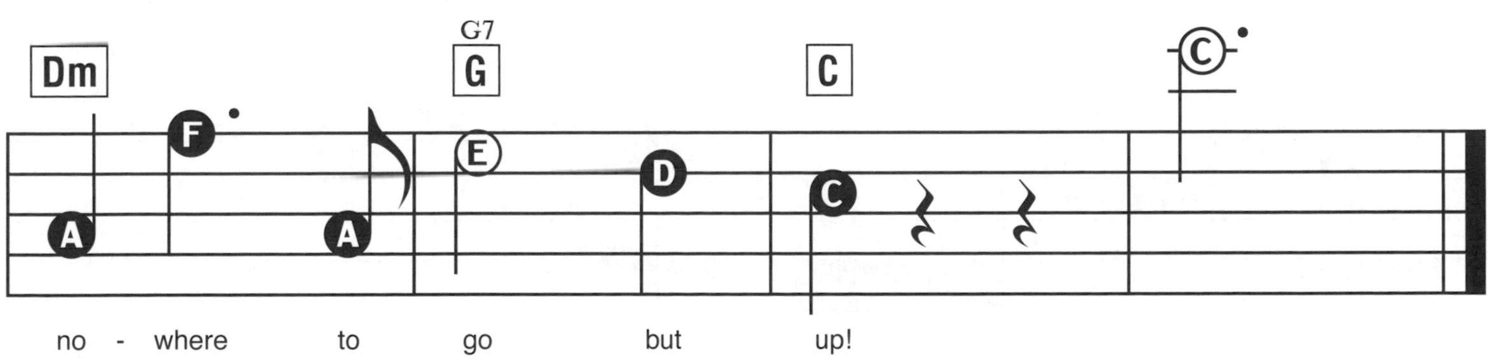
Dm
G7
G
C
A
F
A
E
D
C
C
no - where to go but up!

The Royal Doulton Music Hall

Registration 1
Rhythm: 2-Beat or Broadway

Music by Marc Shaiman
Lyrics by Scott Wittman
and Marc Shaiman

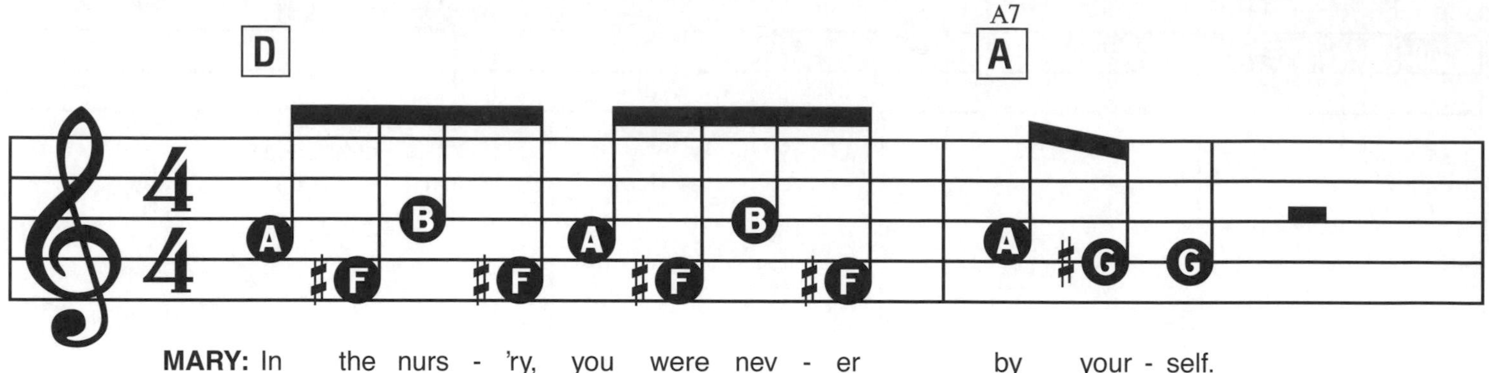
D
A7
A
A
F
B
F
A
F
B
F
A
G
G
MARY: In the nurs - 'ry, you were nev - er by your - self.

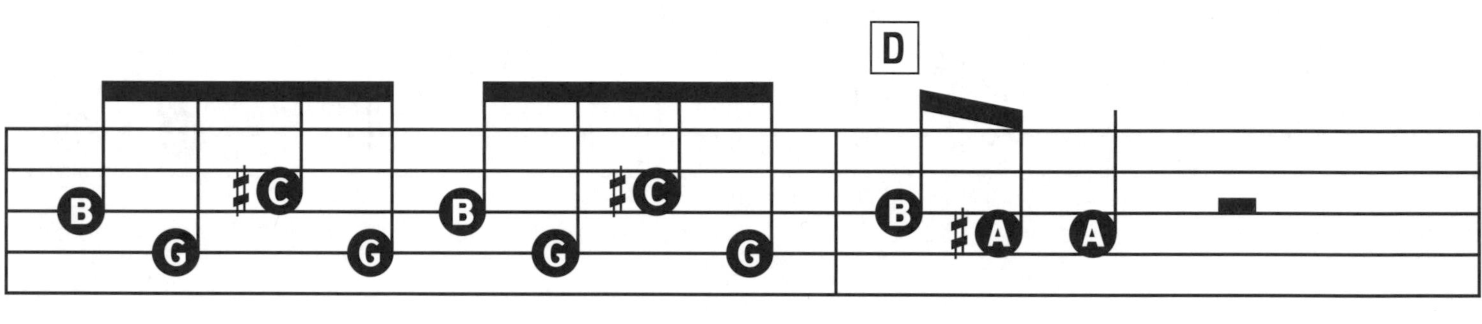
D
B
G
C
G
B
G
C
G
B
A
A
There was quite an - oth - er world up - on your shelf,

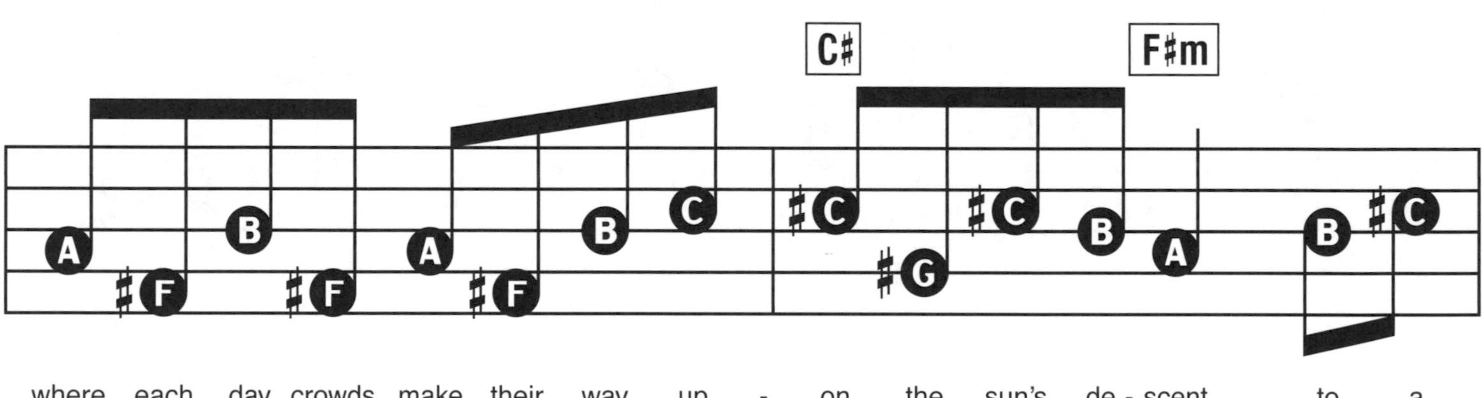
C♯
F♯m
A
F
B
F
A
F
B
C
C
G
C
B
A
B
C
where each day crowds make their way up - on the sun's de - scent to a

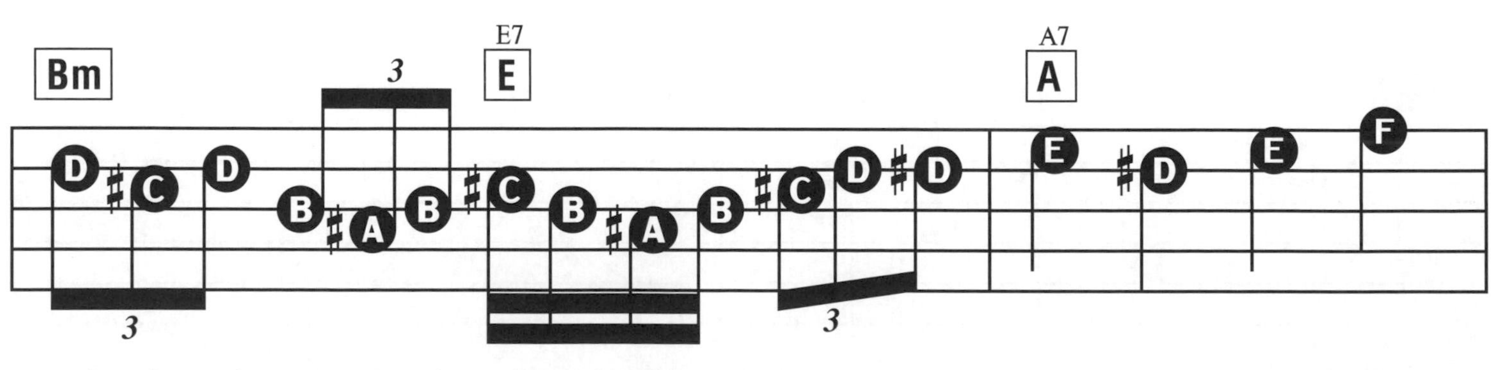
Bm
E7
E
A7
A
3
D
C
D
B
A
B
C
B
A
B
C
D
D
E
D
E
F
myth - i - cal, mys - ti - cal, nev - er quite lo - gis - ti - cal tent! Yes, in this

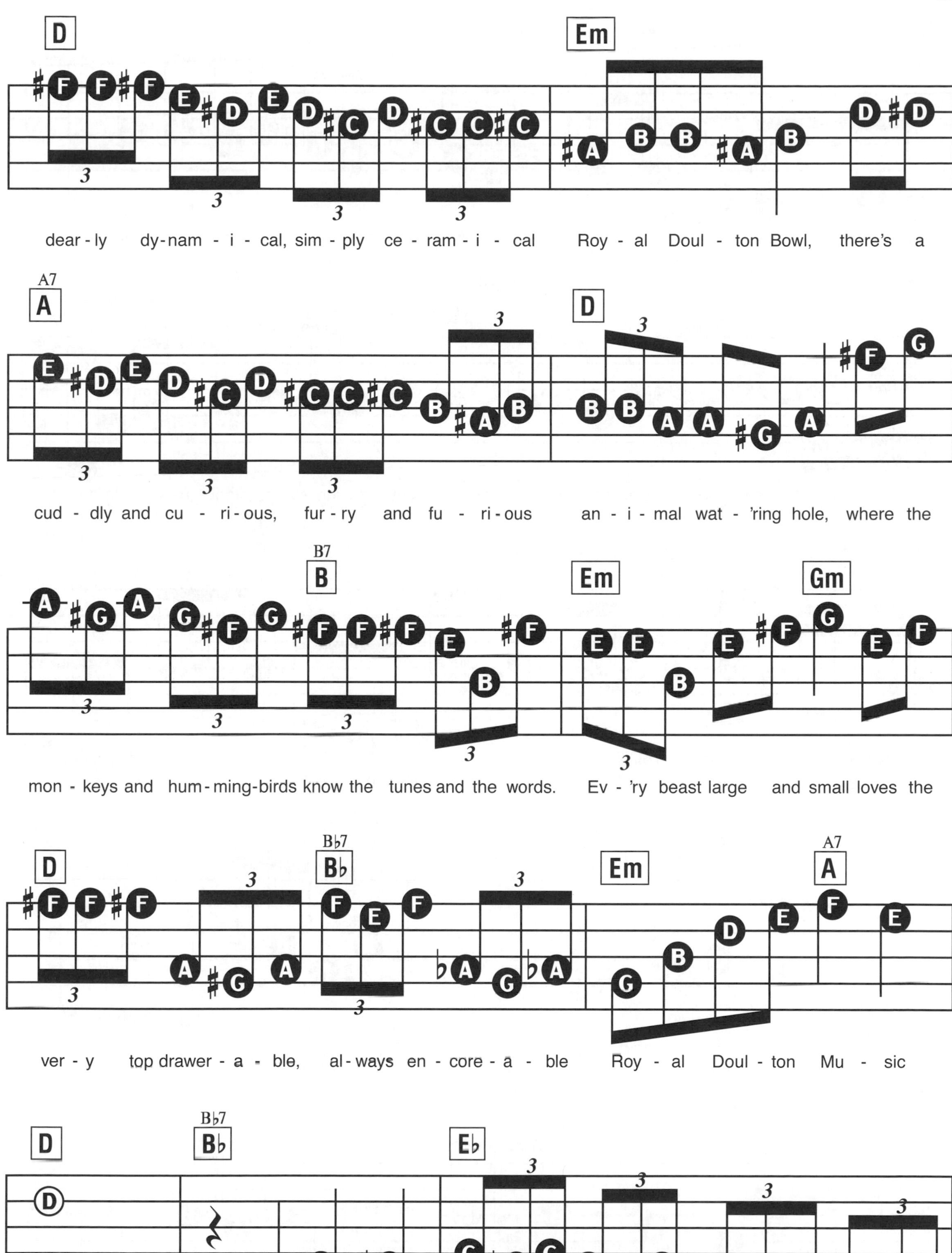
D
Em
dear - ly dy-nam - i - cal, sim - ply ce - ram - i - cal Roy - al Doul - ton Bowl, there's a
A7
A
D
cud - dly and cu - ri - ous, fur - ry and fu - ri - ous an - i - mal wat - 'ring hole, where the
B7
B
Em
Gm
mon - keys and hum - ming-birds know the tunes and the words. Ev - 'ry beast large and small loves the
D
B♭7
B♭
Em
A7
A
ver - y top drawer - a - ble, al - ways en - core - a - ble Roy - al Doul - ton Mu - sic
D
B♭7
B♭
E♭
Hall. Yes, in this mar - vel - ous, mys - ti - cal rath - er so - phis - ti - cal

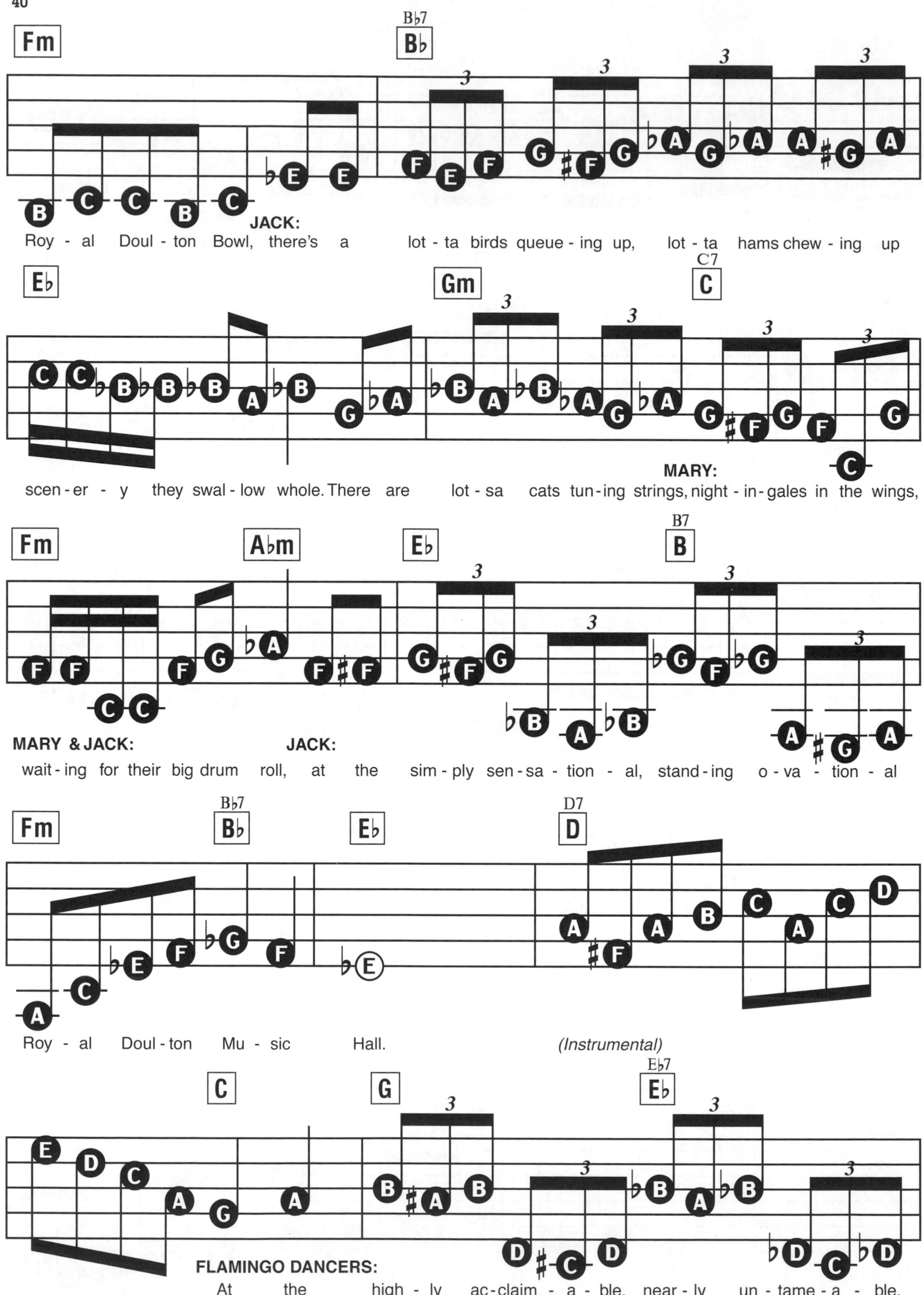
Fm
B♭7
B♭
3
B C C B C ♭E E F E F G ♯F G ♭A G ♭A A ♯G A
JACK:
Roy - al Doul - ton Bowl, there's a lot - ta birds queue - ing up, lot - ta hams chew - ing up
E♭
Gm
C7
C
C C ♭B ♭B ♭B A ♭B G ♭A ♭B A ♭B ♭A G ♭A G ♯F G F C G
MARY:
scen - er - y they swal - low whole. There are lot - sa cats tun - ing strings, night - in - gales in the wings,
Fm
A♭m
E♭
B7
B
F F C C F G ♭A F ♯F G ♯F G ♭B A ♭B ♭G F ♭G A ♯G A
MARY & JACK:
JACK:
wait - ing for their big drum roll, at the sim - ply sen - sa - tion - al, stand - ing o - va - tion - al
Fm
B♭7
B♭
E♭
D7
D
A C ♭E F ♭G F ♭E A ♯F A B C A C D
Roy - al Doul - ton Mu - sic Hall.
(Instrumental)
C
G
E♭7
E♭
E D C A G A B ♯A B D ♯C D ♭B A ♭B ♭D C ♭D
FLAMINGO DANCERS:
At the high - ly ac - claim - a - ble, near - ly un - tame - a - ble,

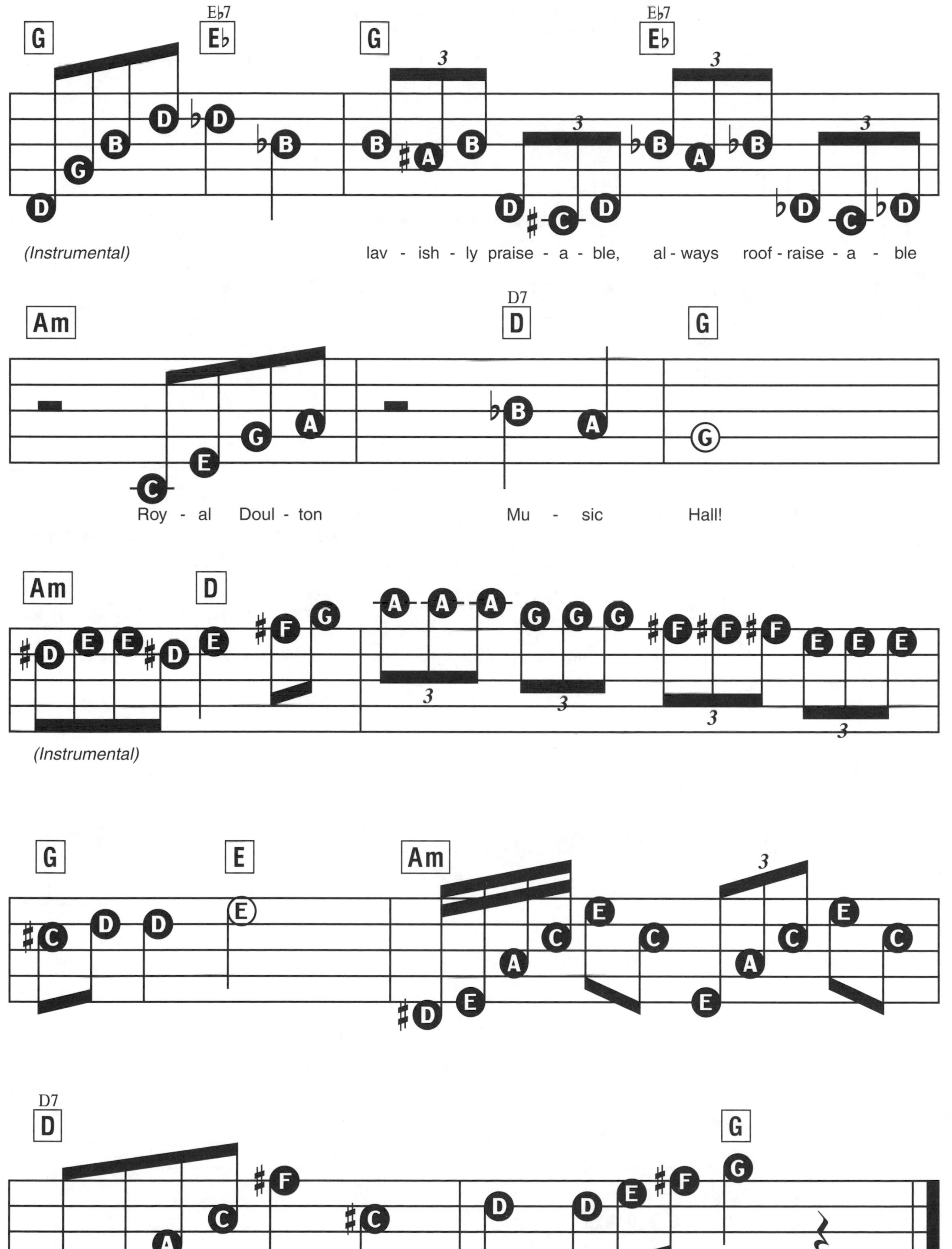
G Eb7 Eb G Eb7 Eb
(Instrumental)
lav - ish - ly praise - a - ble, al - ways roof - raise - a - ble
Am D7 D G
Roy - al Doul - ton Mu - sic Hall!
Am D
(Instrumental)
G E Am
D7 D G

Turning Turtle

Registration 2
Rhythm: None

Music by Marc Shaiman
Lyrics by Scott Wittman
and Marc Shaiman

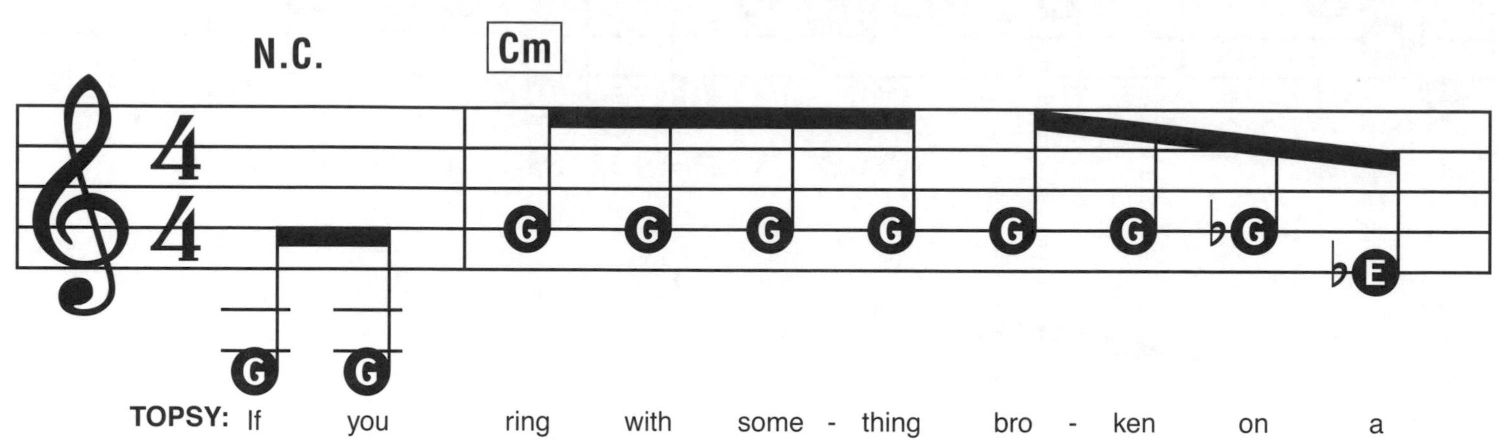

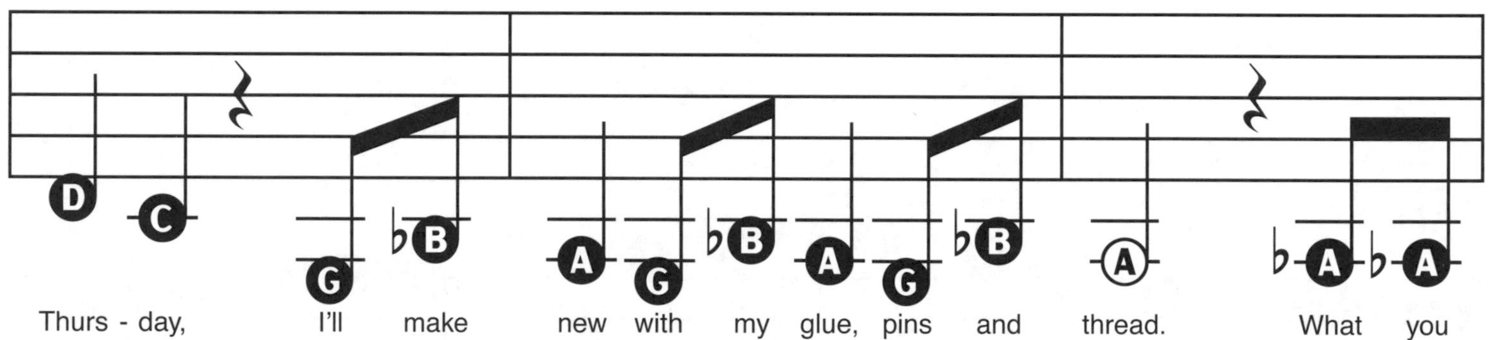

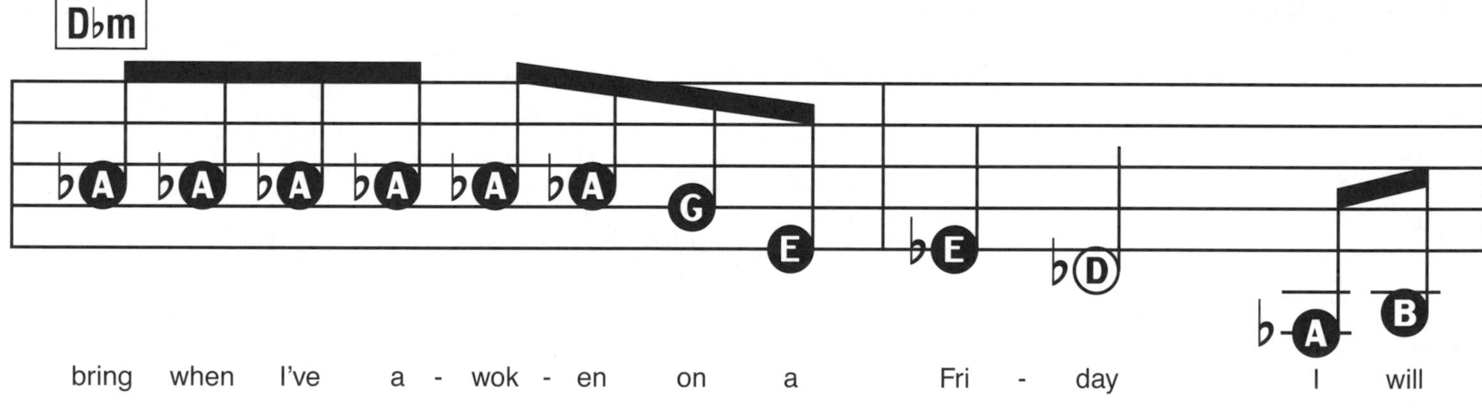

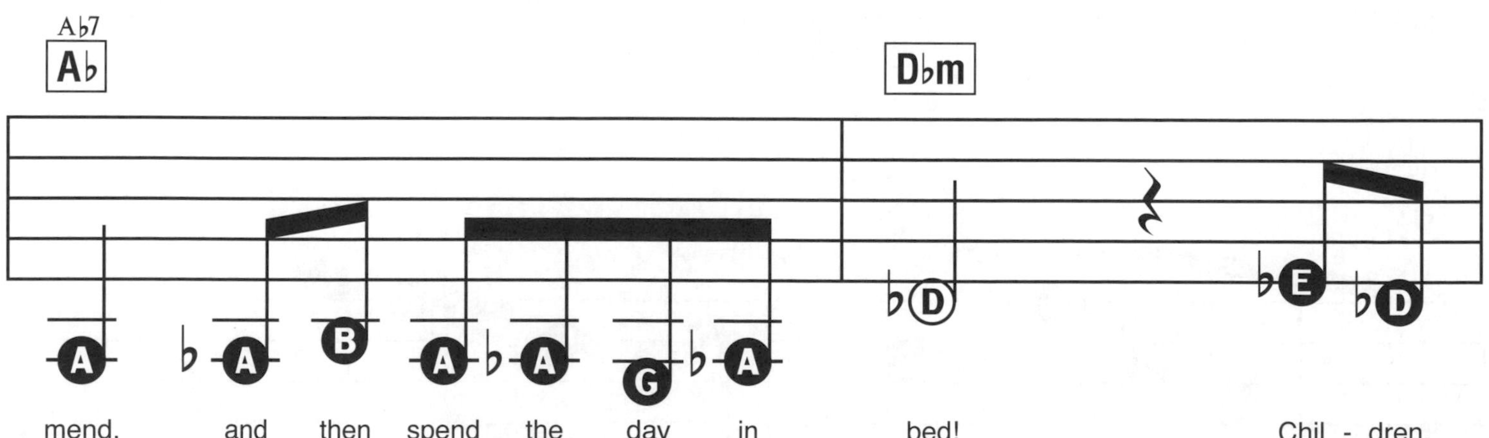

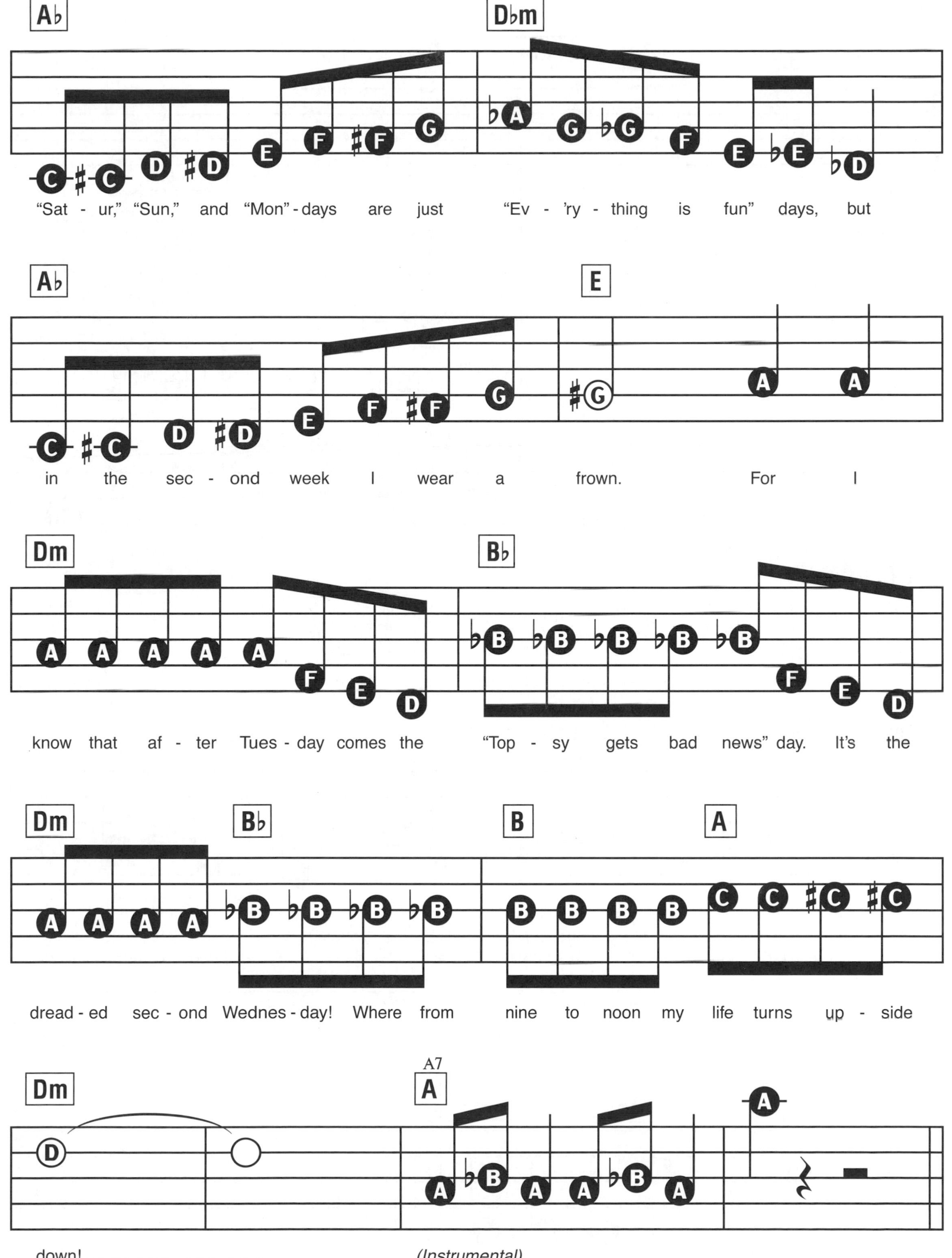
A♭
D♭m
"Sat - ur," "Sun," and "Mon" - days are just "Ev - 'ry - thing is fun" days, but
A♭
E
in the sec - ond week I wear a frown. For I
Dm
B♭
know that af - ter Tues - day comes the "Top - sy gets bad news" day. It's the
Dm
B♭
B
A
dread - ed sec - ond Wednes - day! Where from nine to noon my life turns up - side
Dm
A7
A
down!
(Instrumental)

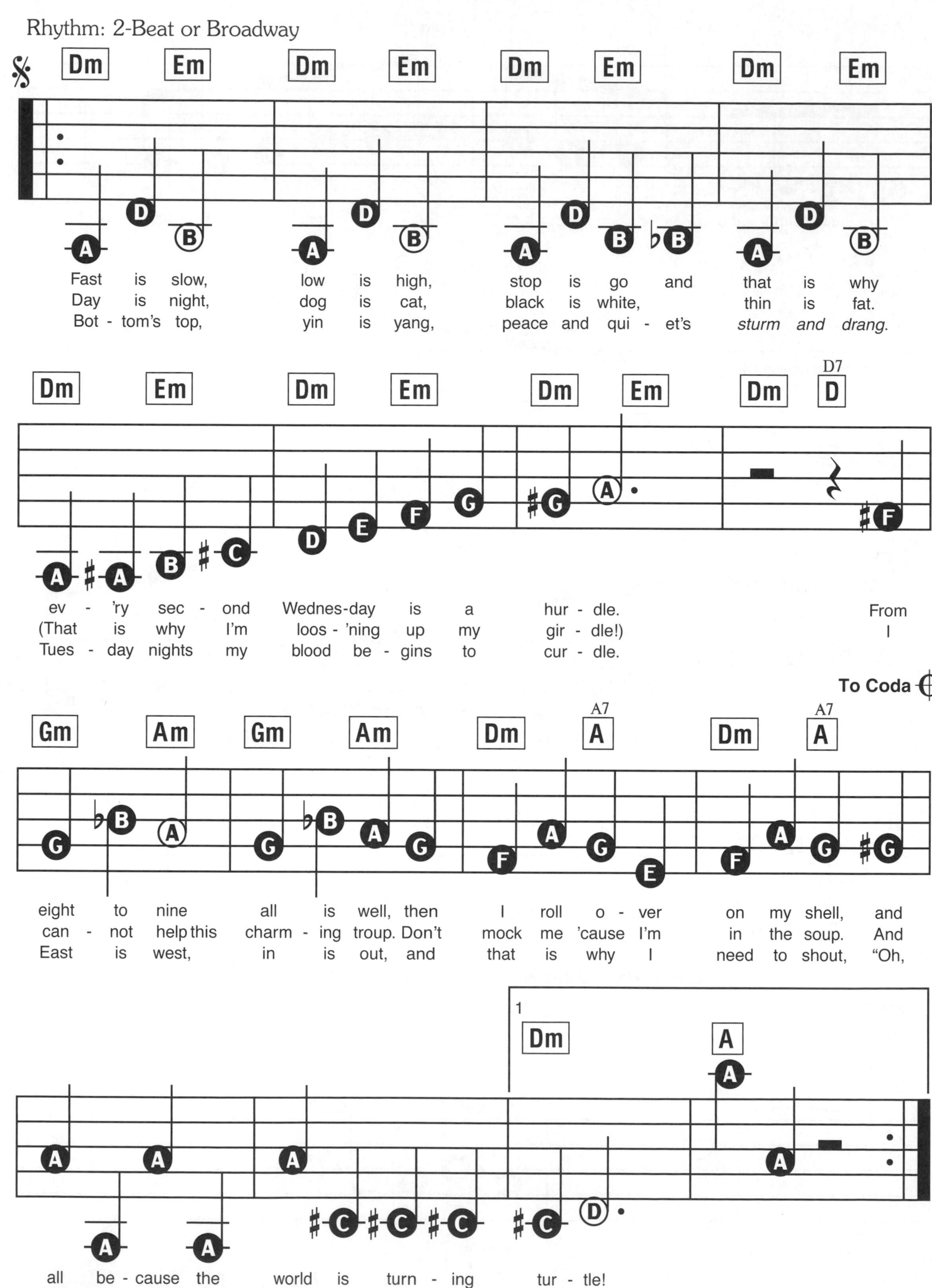
Rhythm: 2-Beat or Broadway
Dm Em Dm Em Dm Em Dm Em
Fast is slow, low is high, stop is go and that is why
Day is night, dog is cat, black is white, thin is fat.
Bot - tom's top, yin is yang, peace and qui - et's sturm and drang.
Dm Em Dm Em Dm Em Dm D7 D
ev - 'ry sec - ond Wednes-day is a hur - dle. From
(That is why I'm loos - 'ning up my gir - dle!) I
Tues - day nights my blood be - gins to cur - dle.
To Coda
Gm Am Gm Am Dm A7 A Dm A7 A
eight to nine all is well, then I roll o - ver on my shell, and
can - not help this charm - ing troup. Don't mock me 'cause I'm in the soup. And
East is west, in is out, and that is why I need to shout, "Oh,
1
Dm A
all be - cause the world is turn - ing tur - tle!
why? Be - cause the world is turn - ing

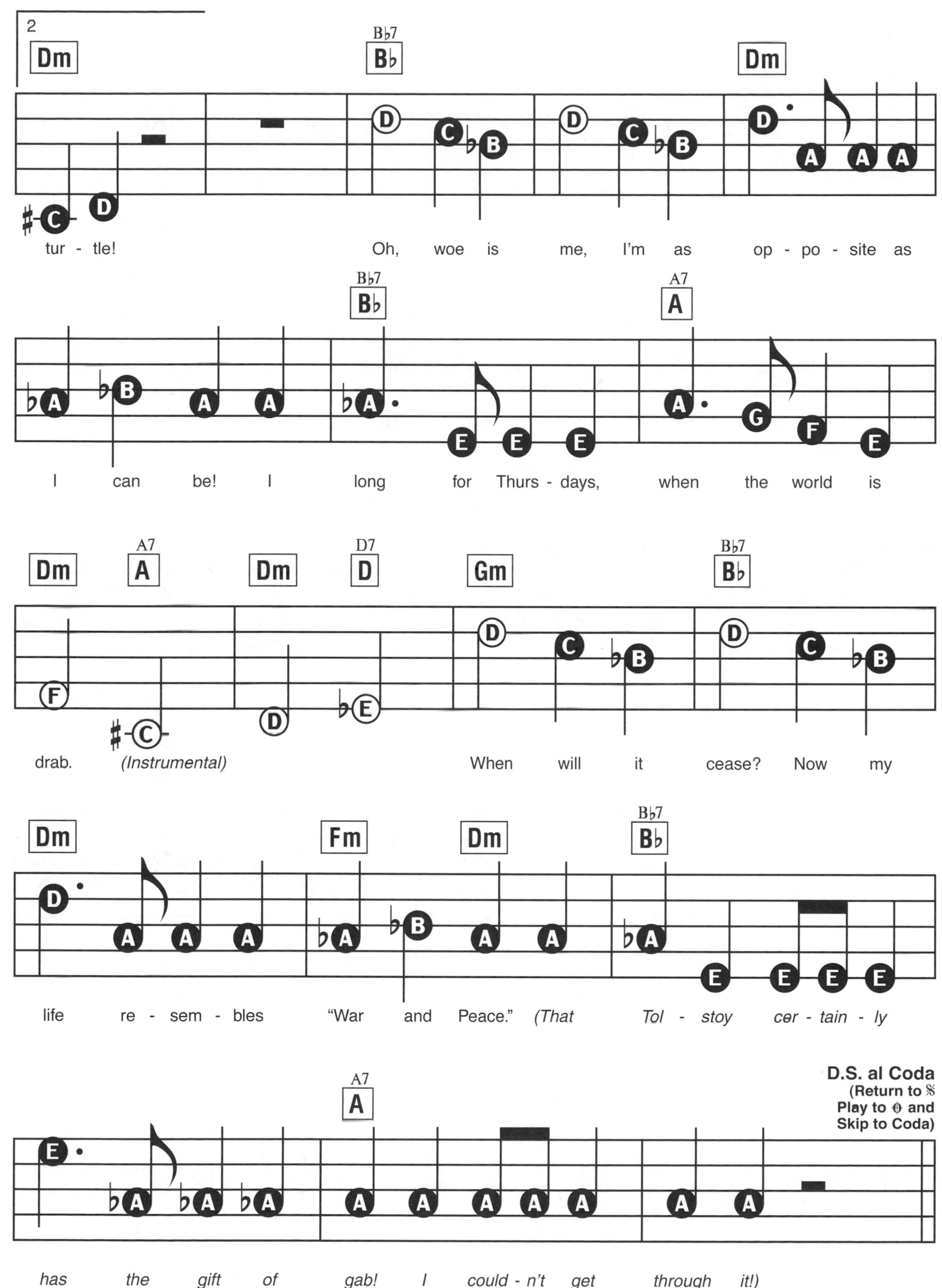
2
Dm
B♭7
B♭
Dm
tur - tle!
Oh, woe is me, I'm as op - po - site as
B♭7
B♭
A7
A
I can be! I long for Thurs - days, when the world is
Dm
A7
A
Dm
D7
D
Gm
B♭7
B♭
drab. (Instrumental)
When will it cease? Now my
Dm
Fm
Dm
B♭7
B♭
life re - sem - bles "War and Peace." (That Tol - stoy cer - tain - ly
A7
A
D.S. al Coda
(Return to 𝄋
Play to ⊕ and
Skip to Coda)
has the gift of gab! I could - n't get through it!)

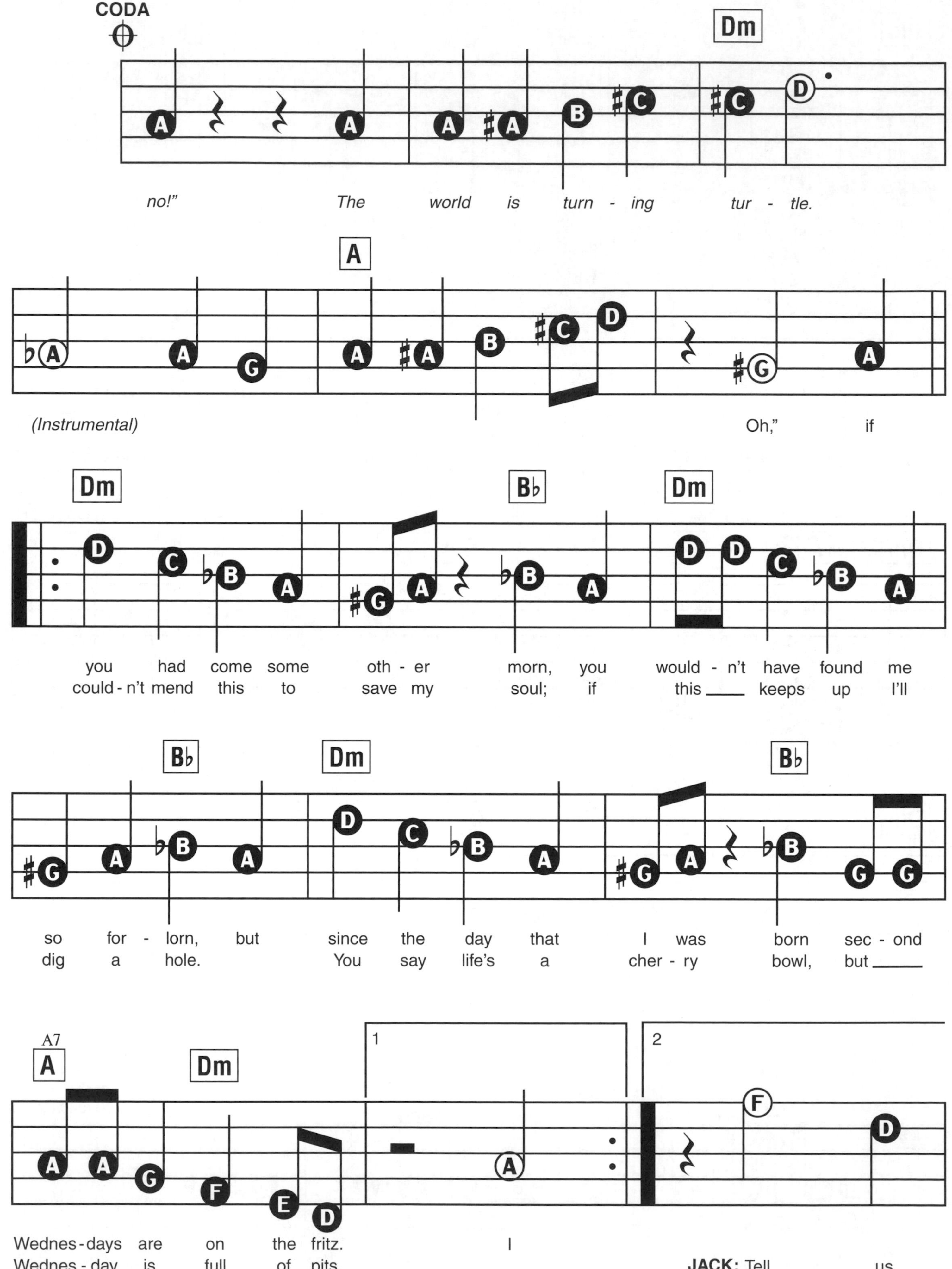
CODA
Dm
no!" The world is turn - ing tur - tle.
A
(Instrumental)
Oh," if
Dm
Bb
Dm
you had come some oth - er morn, you would - n't have found me
could - n't mend this to save my soul; if this keeps up I'll
Bb
Dm
Bb
so for - lorn, but since the day that I was born sec - ond
dig a hole. You say life's a cher - ry bowl, but
A7
A
Dm
1
2
Wednes - days are on the fritz. I
Wednes - day is full of pits.
JACK: Tell us,

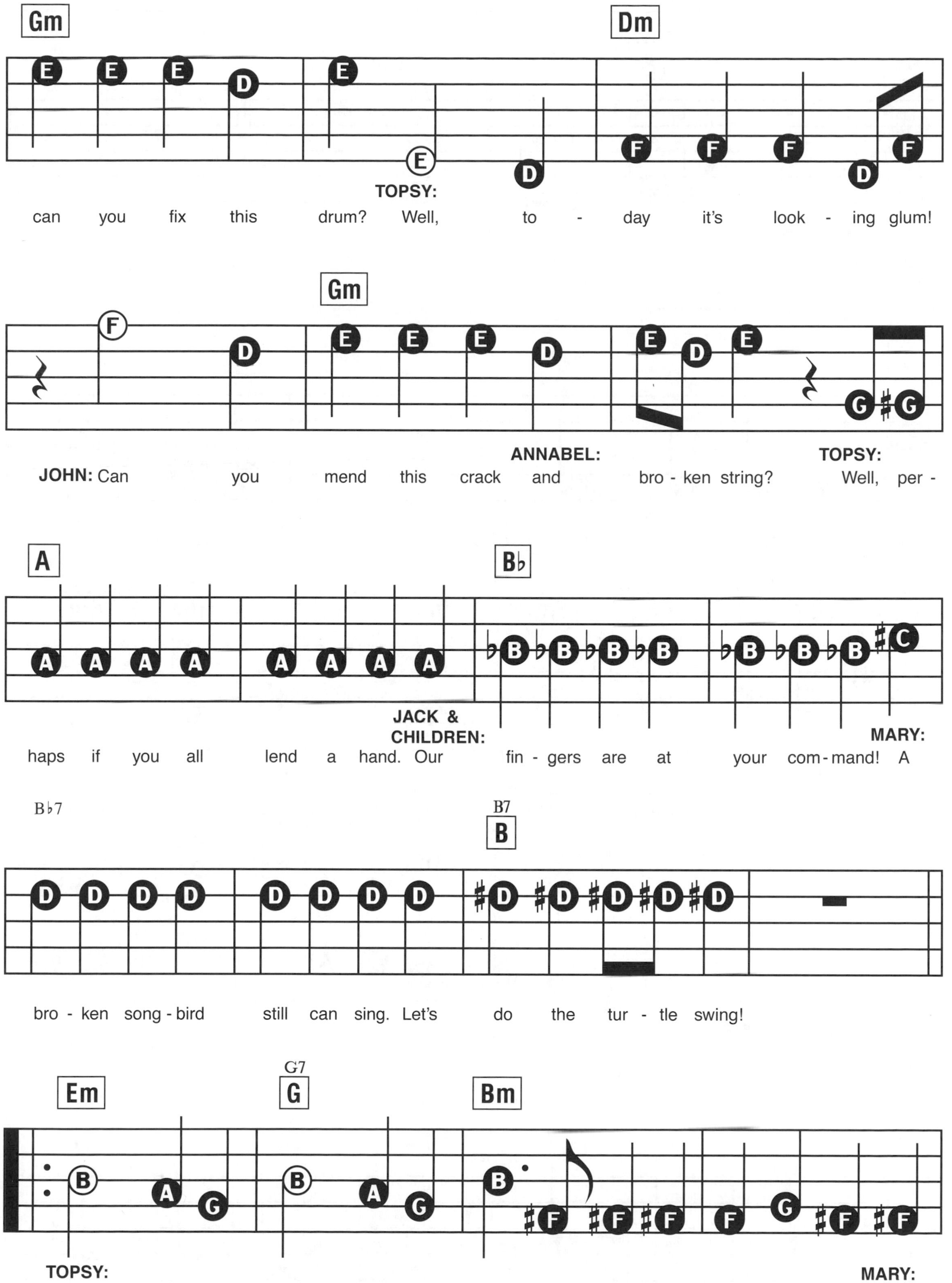

Gm
Dm
TOPSY:
can you fix this drum? Well, to - day it's look - ing glum!
Gm
JOHN: Can you mend this crack and
ANNABEL:
bro - ken string?
TOPSY:
Well, per -
A
B♭
JACK & CHILDREN:
haps if you all lend a hand. Our fin - gers are at your com - mand!
MARY:
A
B♭7
B7
B
bro - ken song - bird still can sing. Let's do the tur - tle swing!
Em
G7
G
Bm
TOPSY:
Oh, woe is me. Now I'm on my head. How can it be?
Here on your head, "a" is far be - hind and led by "zed."
MARY:
Well, It's

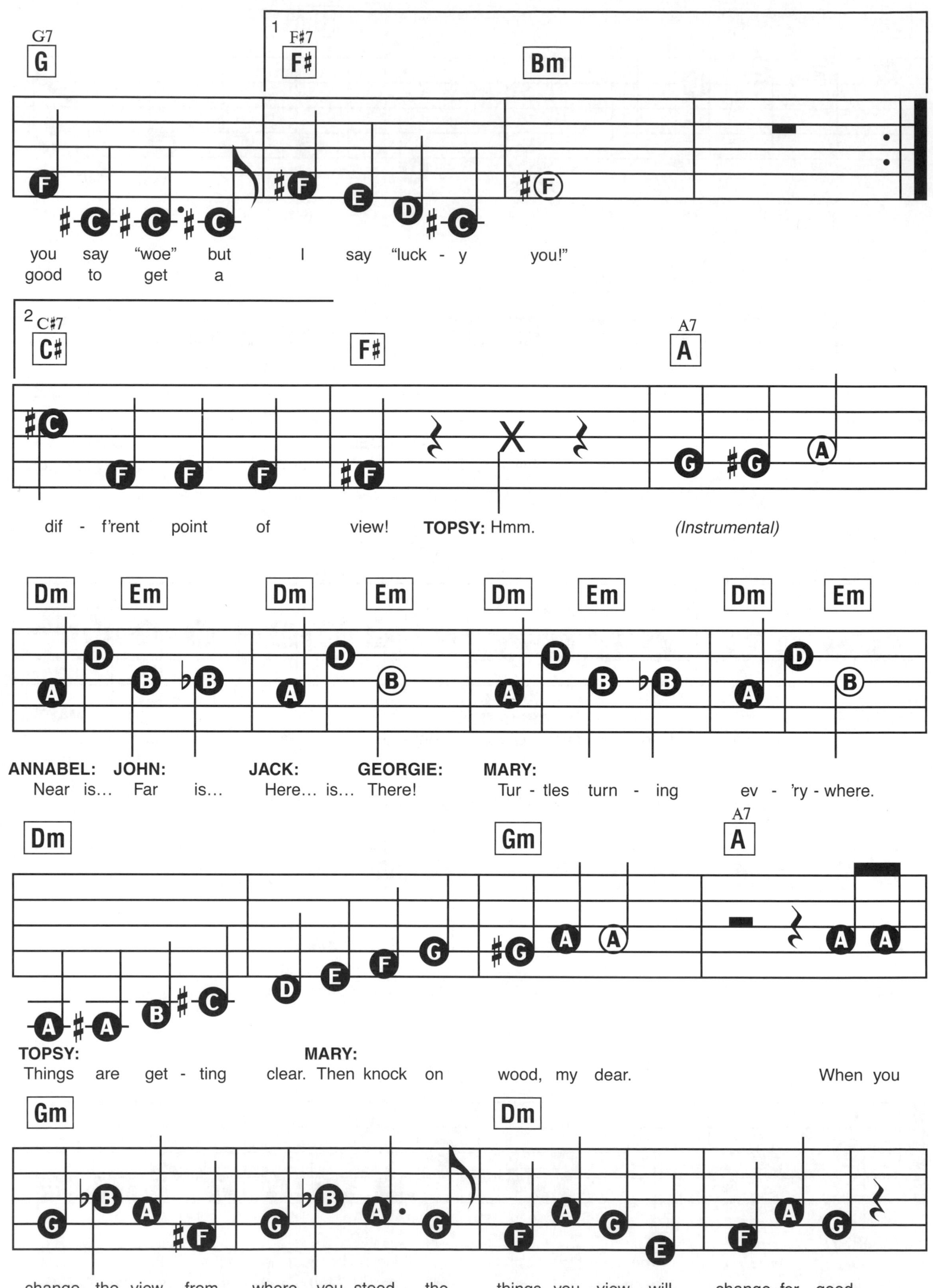
G7
G
1
F#7
F♯
Bm
you say "woe" but I say "luck - y you!"
good to get a
2
C#7
C♯
F♯
A7
A
dif - f'rent point of view! TOPSY: Hmm.
(Instrumental)
Dm
Em
ANNABEL: JOHN: JACK: GEORGIE: MARY:
Near is... Far is... Here... is... There! Tur - tles turn - ing ev - 'ry - where.
Dm
Gm
A7
A
TOPSY:
Things are get - ting clear. Then knock on wood, my dear. When you
MARY:
Gm
Dm
change the view from where you stood, the things you view will change for good.

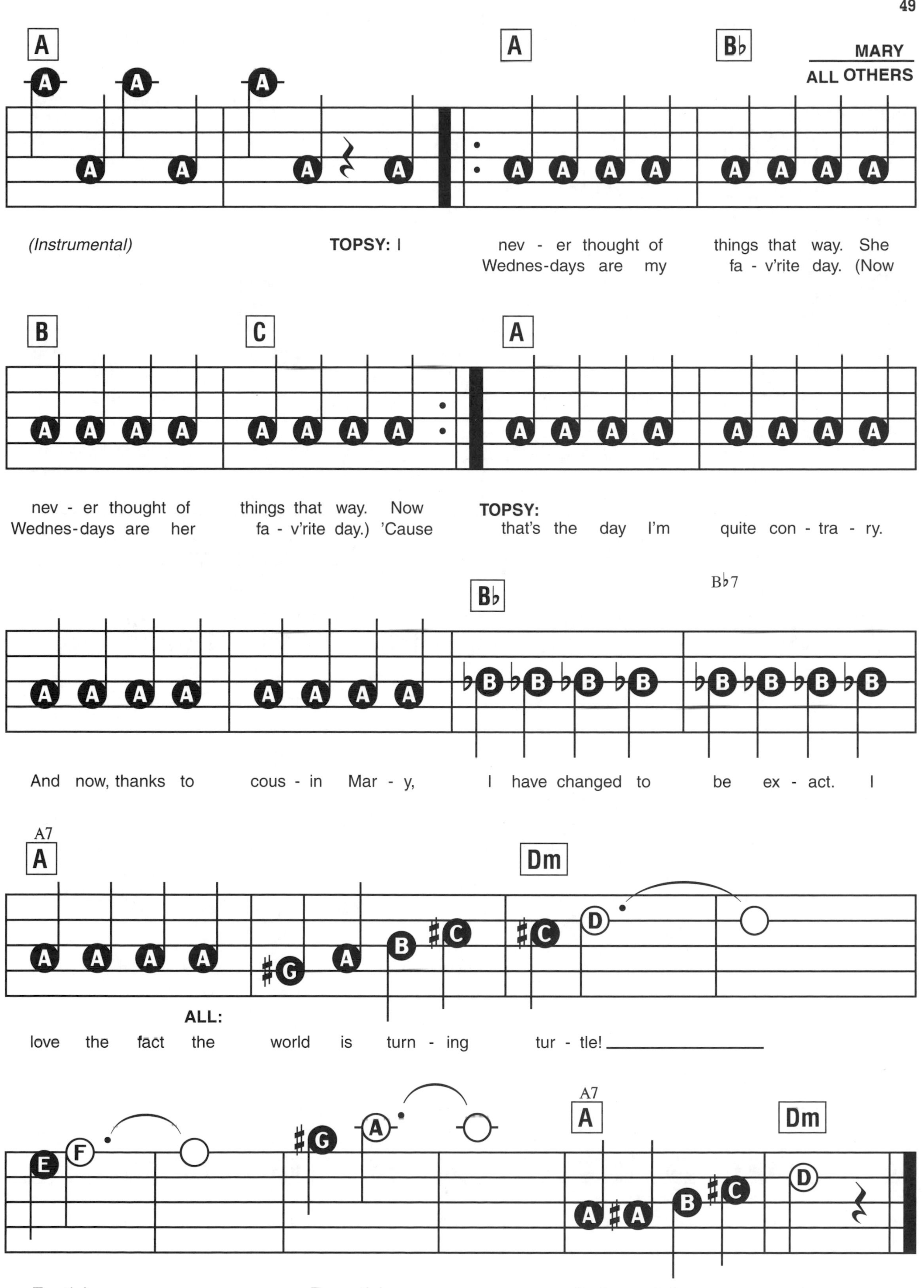
A
A
A
A
A
A
A
A
MARY
ALL OTHERS
A A A A
Bb
A A A A
(Instrumental)
TOPSY: I
nev - er thought of
Wednes-days are my
things that way. She
fa - v'rite day. (Now
B
A A A A
C
A A A A
A
A A A A
A A A A
nev - er thought of
Wednes-days are her
things that way. Now
fa - v'rite day.) 'Cause
TOPSY:
that's the day I'm
quite con - tra - ry.
A A A A
A A A A
Bb
Bb7
B B B B
B B B B
And now, thanks to
cous - in Mar - y,
I have changed to
be ex - act. I
A7
A
A A A A
G A B C
Dm
C D
ALL:
love the fact the
world is turn - ing
tur - tle!
E F
G A
A7
A
A A B C
Dm
D
Tur-tle!
Tur - tle!
(Instrumental)

Trip a Little Light Fantastic

Registration 1
Rhythm: 2-Beat or Broadway

Music by Marc Shaiman
Lyrics by Scott Wittman
and Marc Shaiman

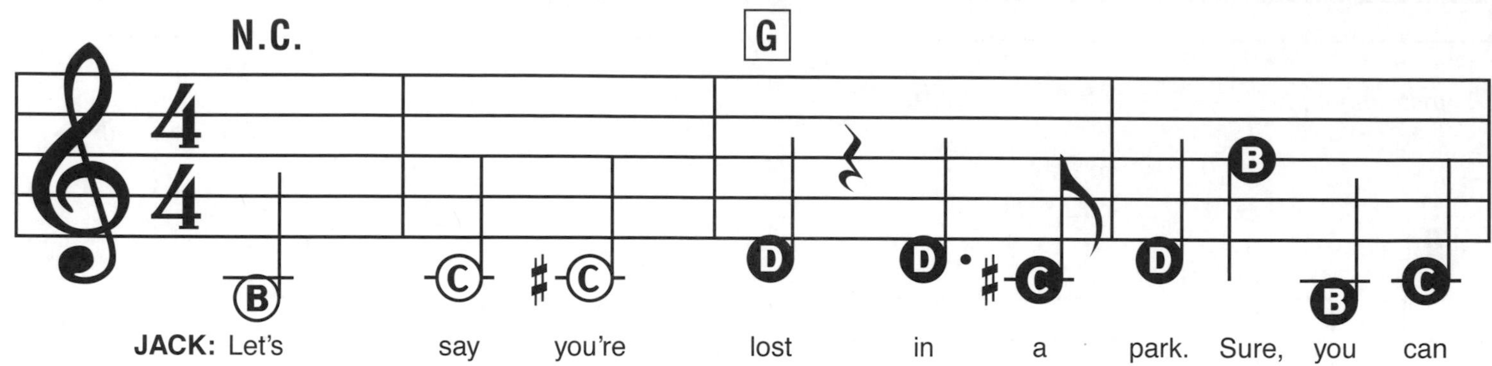
N.C.
G
B C C D D C D B B C
JACK: Let's say you're lost in a park. Sure, you can

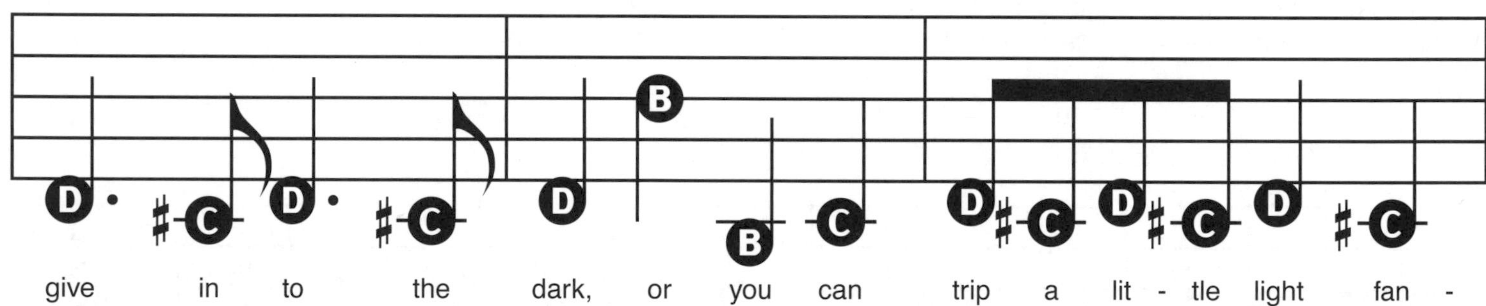
D C D C D B B C D C D C D C
give in to the dark, or you can trip a lit - tle light fan -

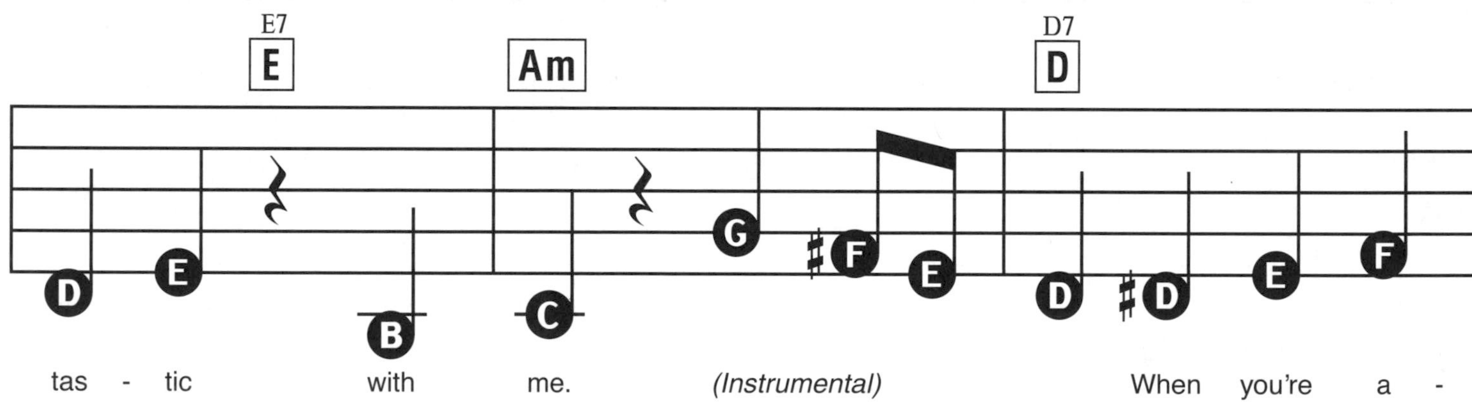
E7
E
Am
D7
D
D E B C G F E D D E F
tas - tic with me. (Instrumental) When you're a -

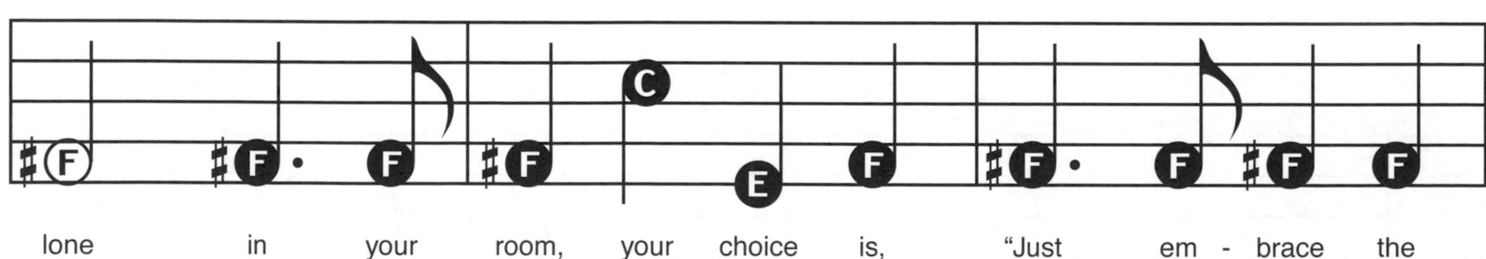
F F F F C E F F F F F
lone in your room, your choice is, "Just em - brace the

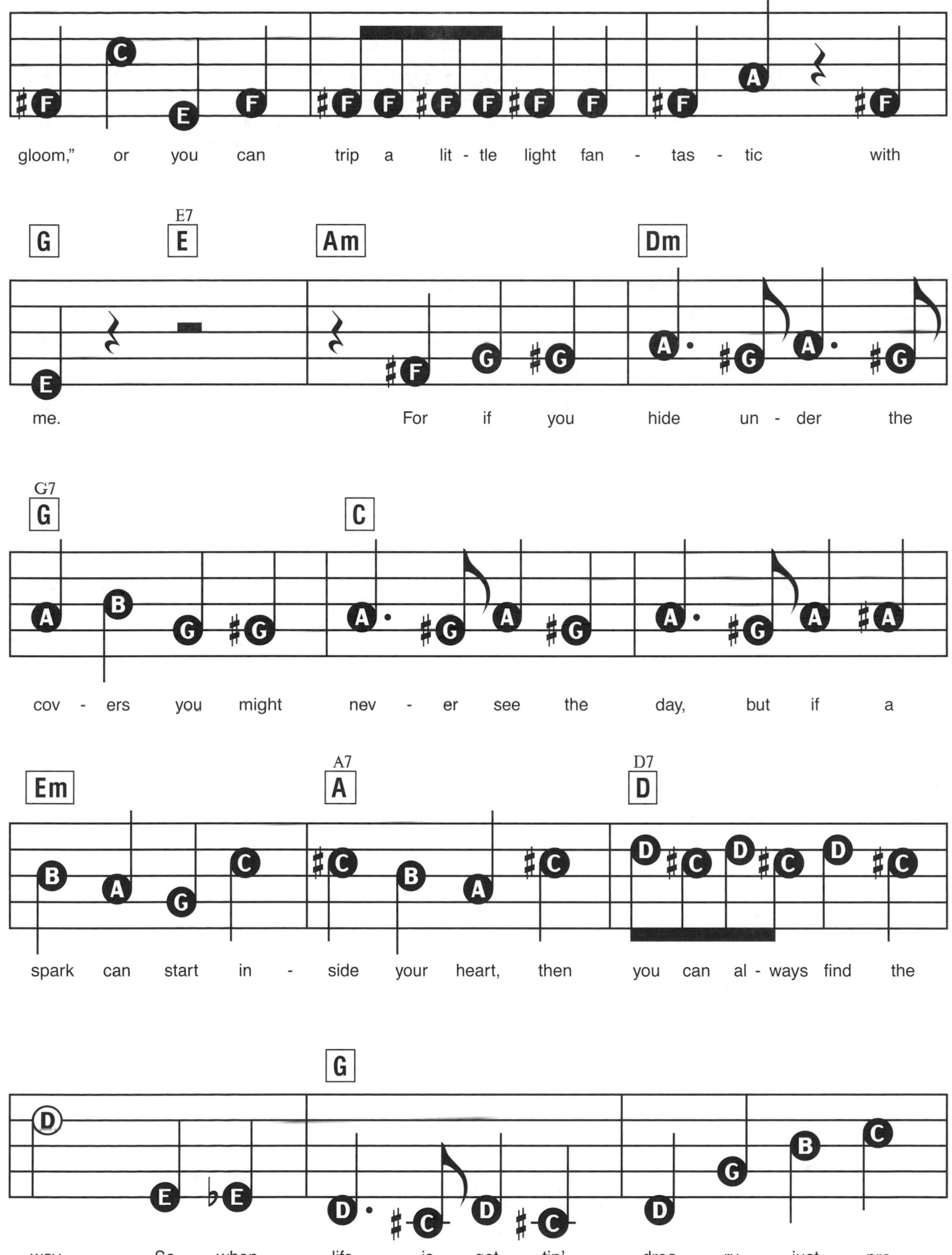
gloom," or you can trip a lit - tle light fan - tas - tic with
G E7 E Am Dm
me. For if you hide un - der the
G7 G C
cov - ers you might nev - er see the day, but if a
Em A7 A D7 D
spark can start in - side your heart, then you can al - ways find the
G
way. So when life is get - tin' drea - ry, just pre -

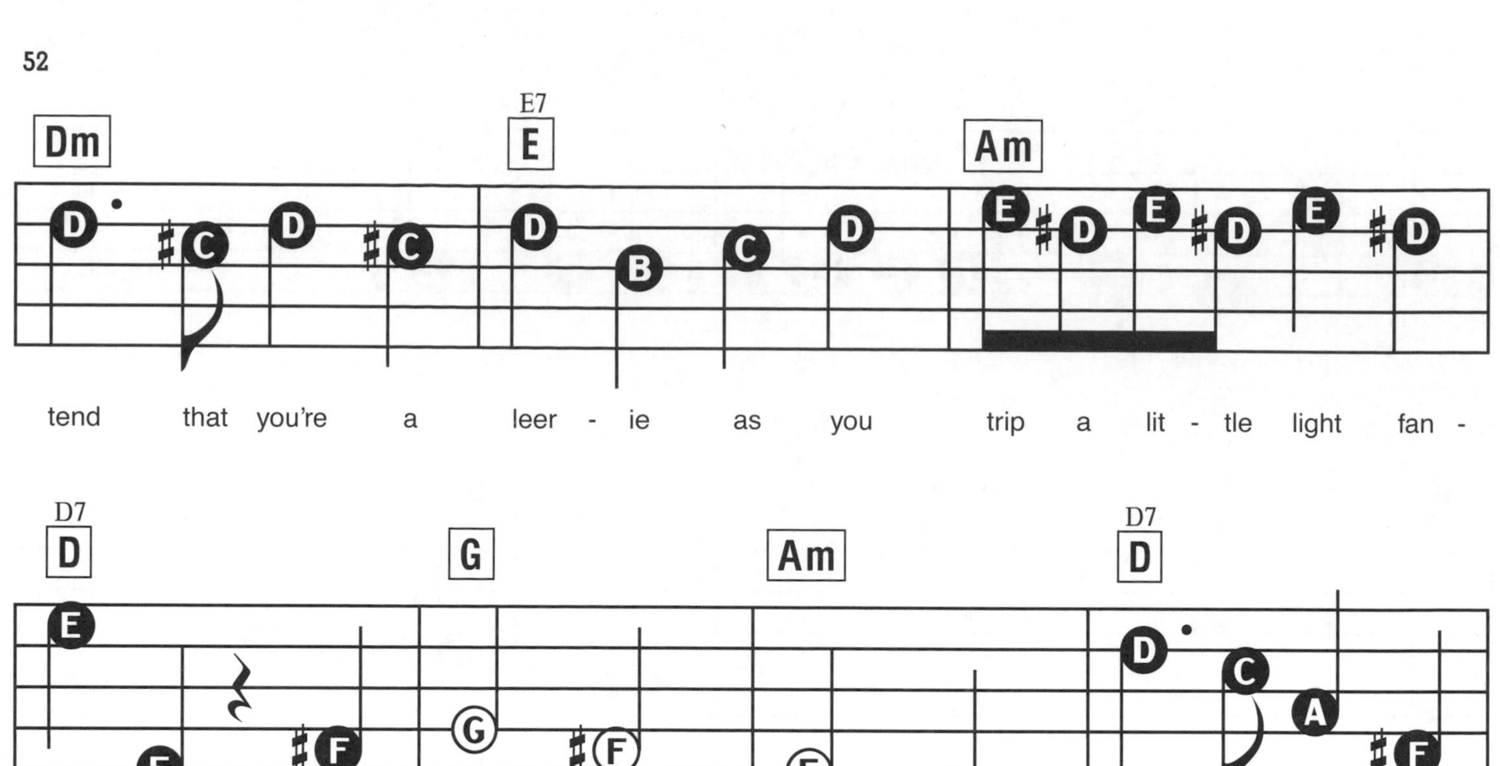

Dm
E7
E
Am
tend that you're a leer - ie as you trip a lit - tle light fan -

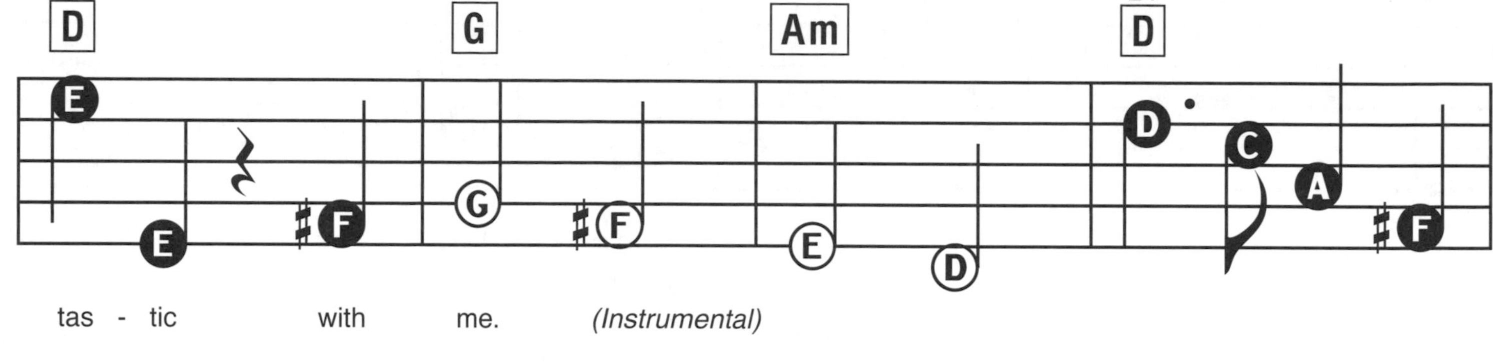

D7
D
G
Am
D7
D
tas - tic with me. (Instrumental)

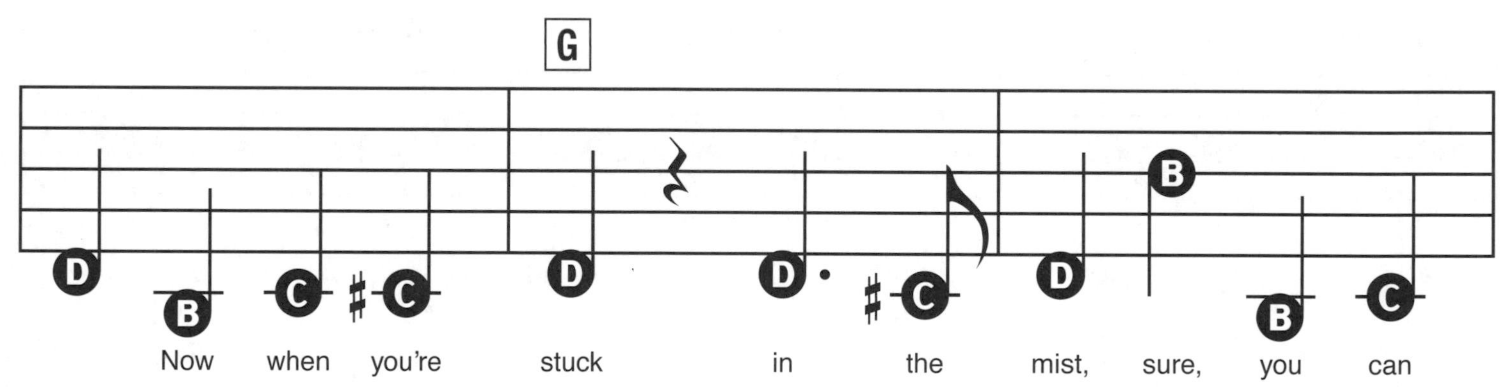

G
Now when you're stuck in the mist, sure, you can

strug - gle and re - sist, or you can trip a lit - tle light fan -

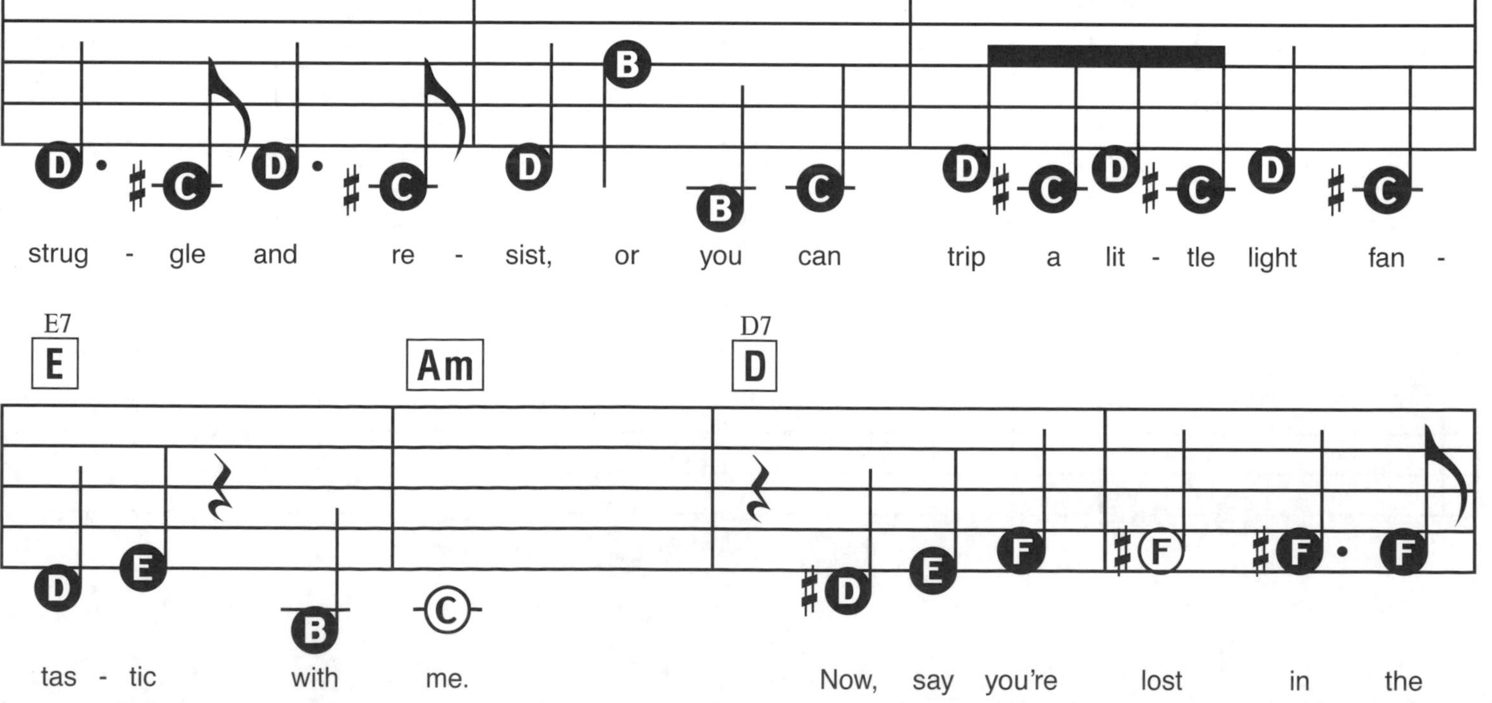

E7
E
Am
D7
D
tas - tic with me. Now, say you're lost in the

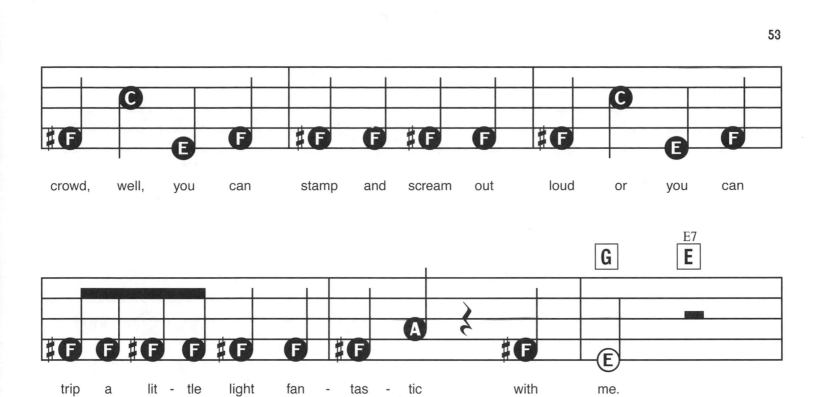

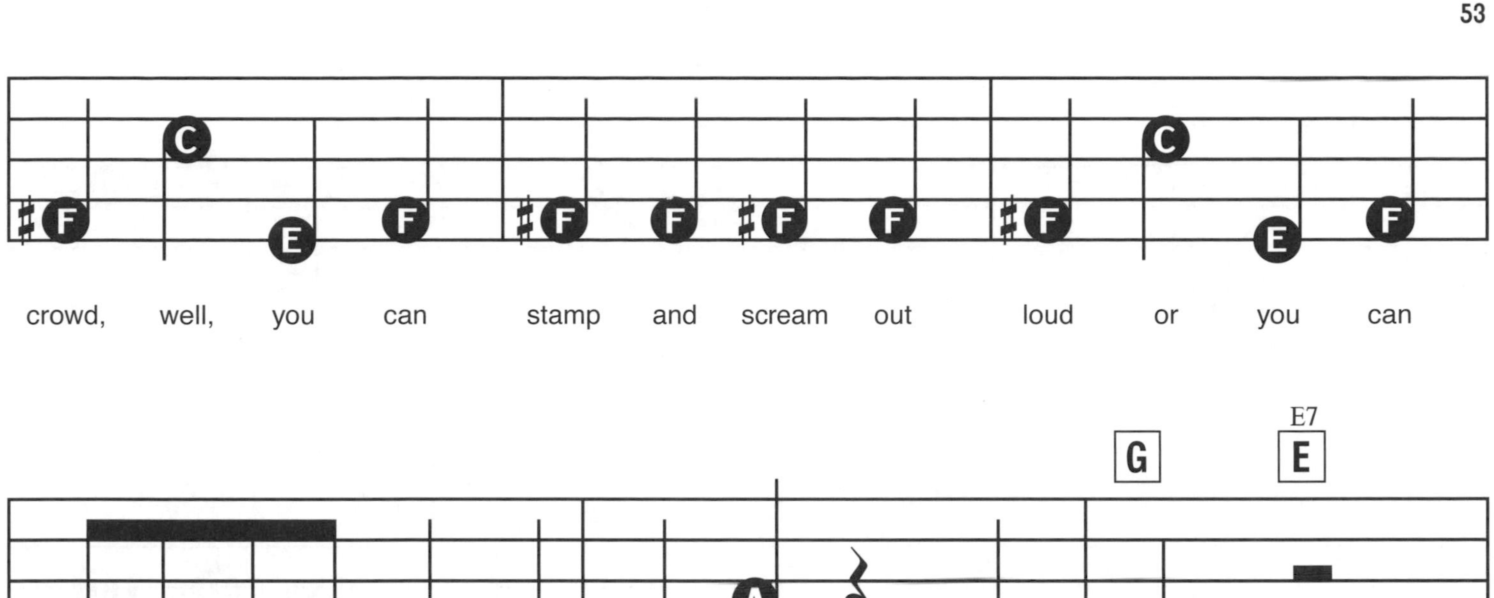
C
F
E
F
F
F
F
F
F
C
E
F
crowd, well, you can stamp and scream out loud or you can

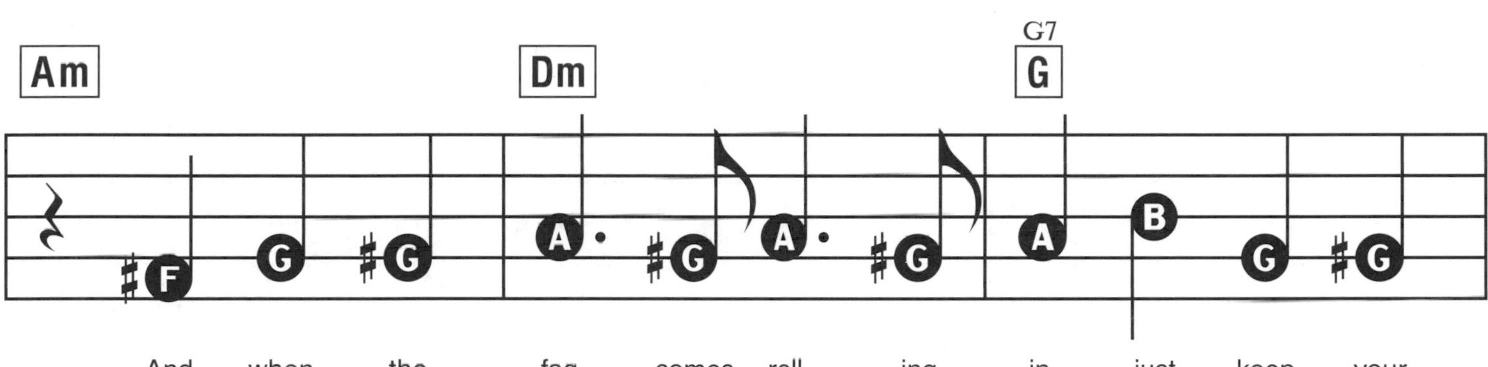
G
E7
E
F
F
F
F
F
F
F
A
F
E
trip a lit - tle light fan - tas - tic with me.

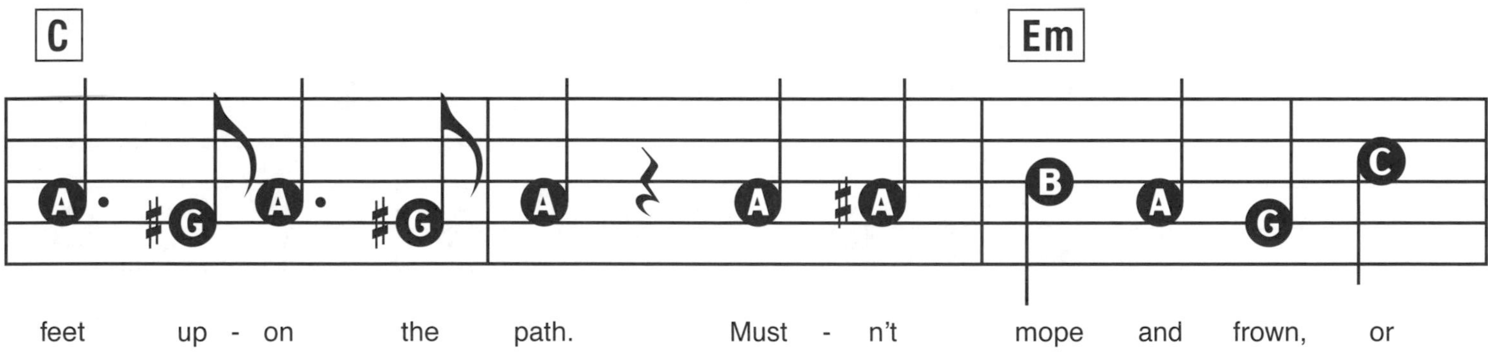
Am
Dm
G7
G
F
G
G
A
G
A
G
A
B
G
G
And when the fog comes roll - ing in, just keep your
C
Em
A
G
A
G
A
A
A
B
A
G
C
feet up - on the path. Must - n't mope and frown, or

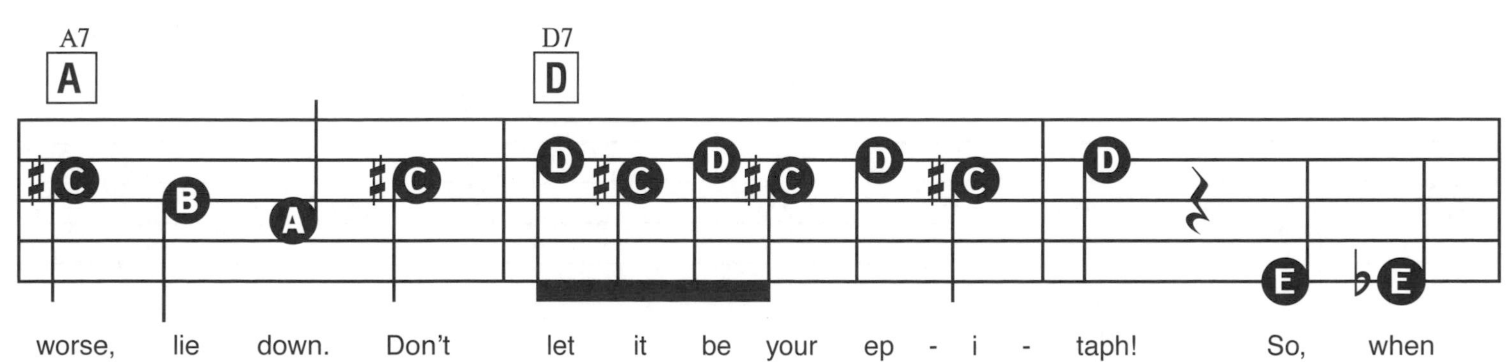
A7
A
D7
D
C
B
A
C
D
C
D
C
D
C
D
E
E
worse, lie down. Don't let it be your ep - i - taph! So, when

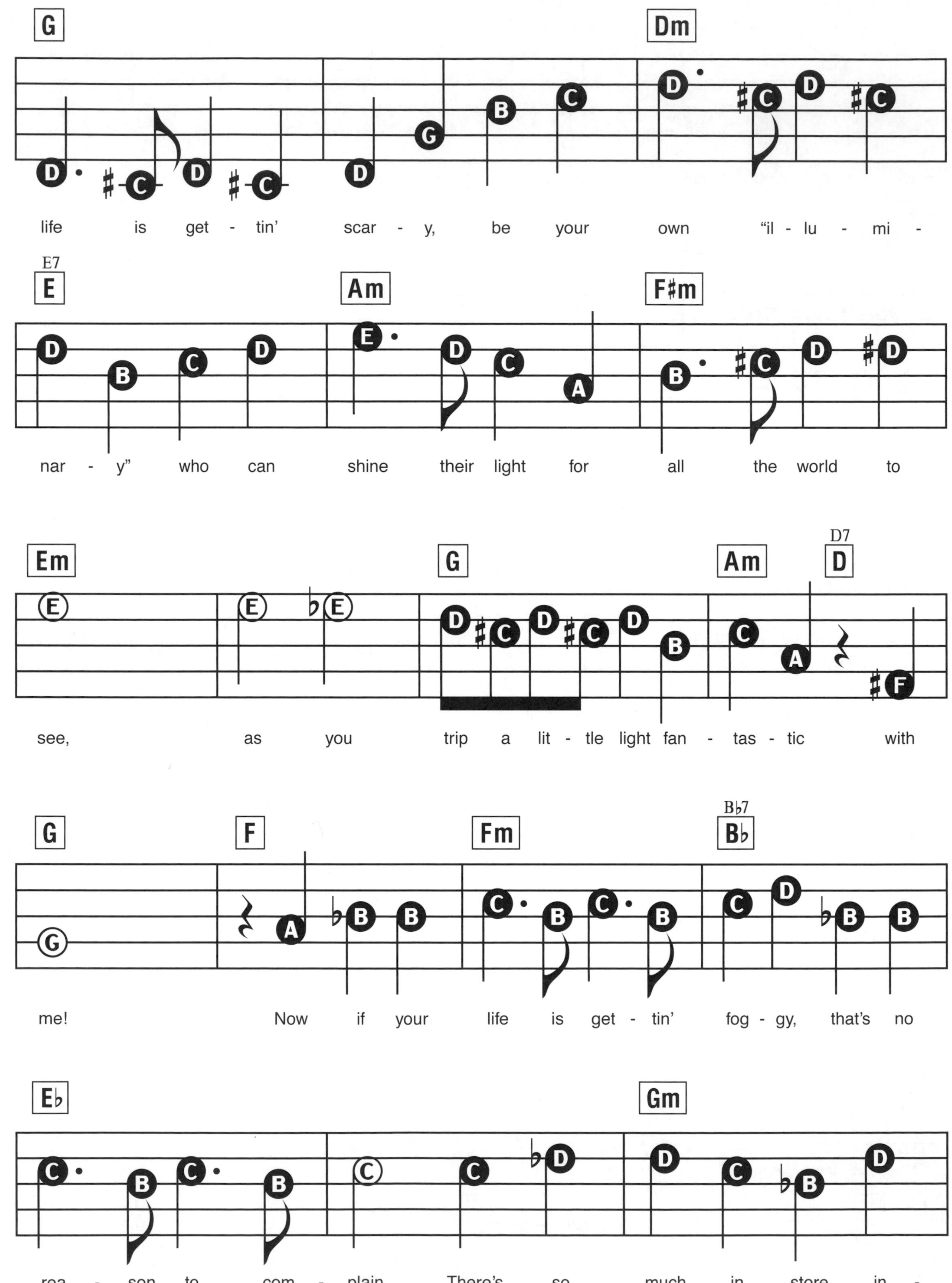
G
Dm
life is get - tin' scar - y, be your own "il - lu - mi -
E7
E
Am
F♯m
nar - y" who can shine their light for all the world to
Em
G
Am
D7
D
see, as you trip a lit - tle light fan - tas - tic with
G
F
Fm
B♭7
B♭
me! Now if your life is get - tin' fog - gy, that's no
E♭
Gm
rea - son to com - plain. There's so much in store in -

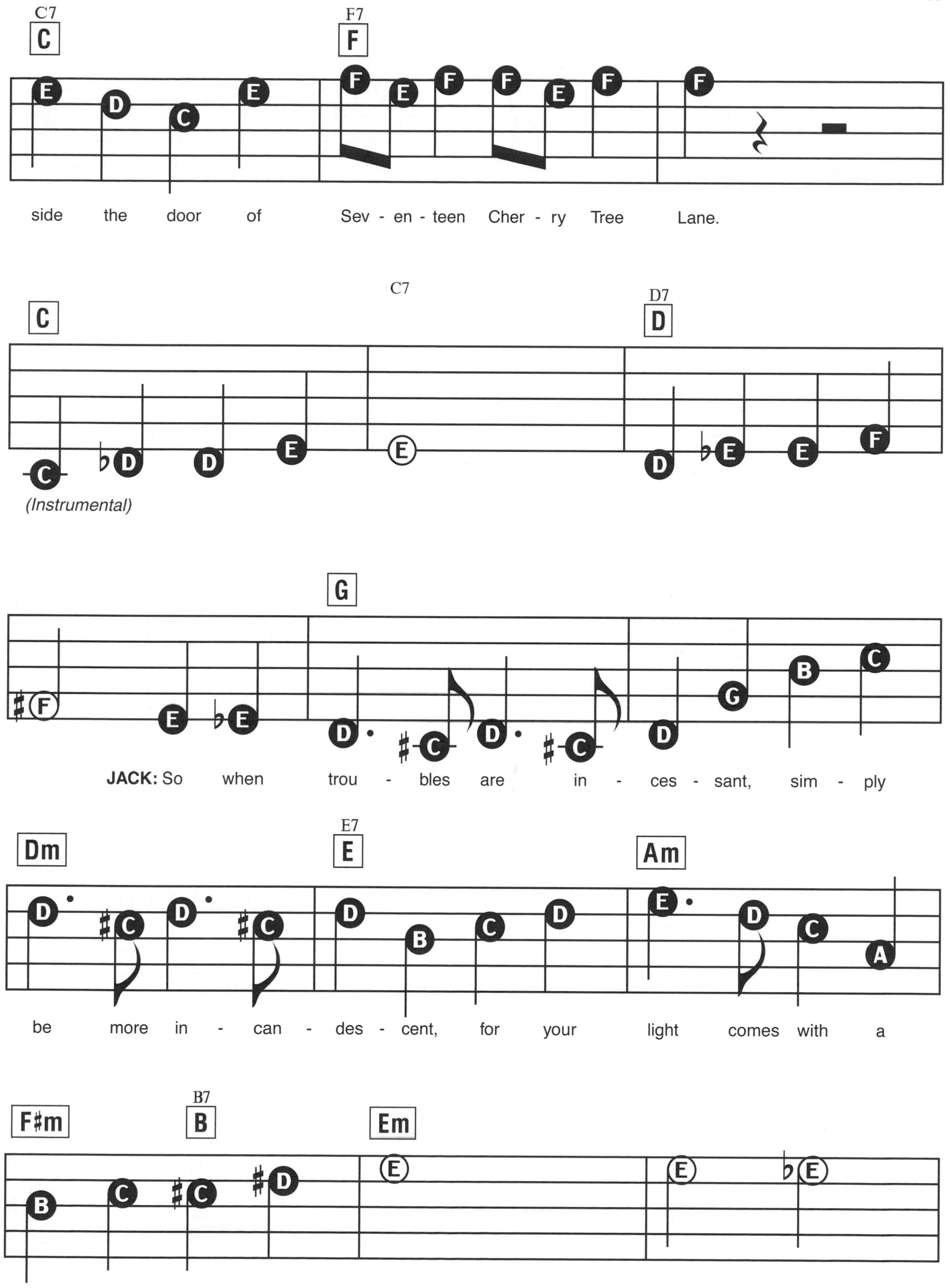
C7
C
F7
F
E D C E F E F F E F F
side the door of Sev - en - teen Cher - ry Tree Lane.
C
C7
D7
D
C ♭D D E E D ♭E E F
(Instrumental)
G
♯F E ♭E D ♯C D ♯C D G B C
JACK: So when trou - bles are in - ces - sant, sim - ply
Dm
E7
E
Am
D ♯C D ♯C D B C D E D C A
be more in - can - des - cent, for your light comes with a
F♯m
B7
B
Em
B C ♯C ♯D E E ♭E
life - time guar - an - tee, as you

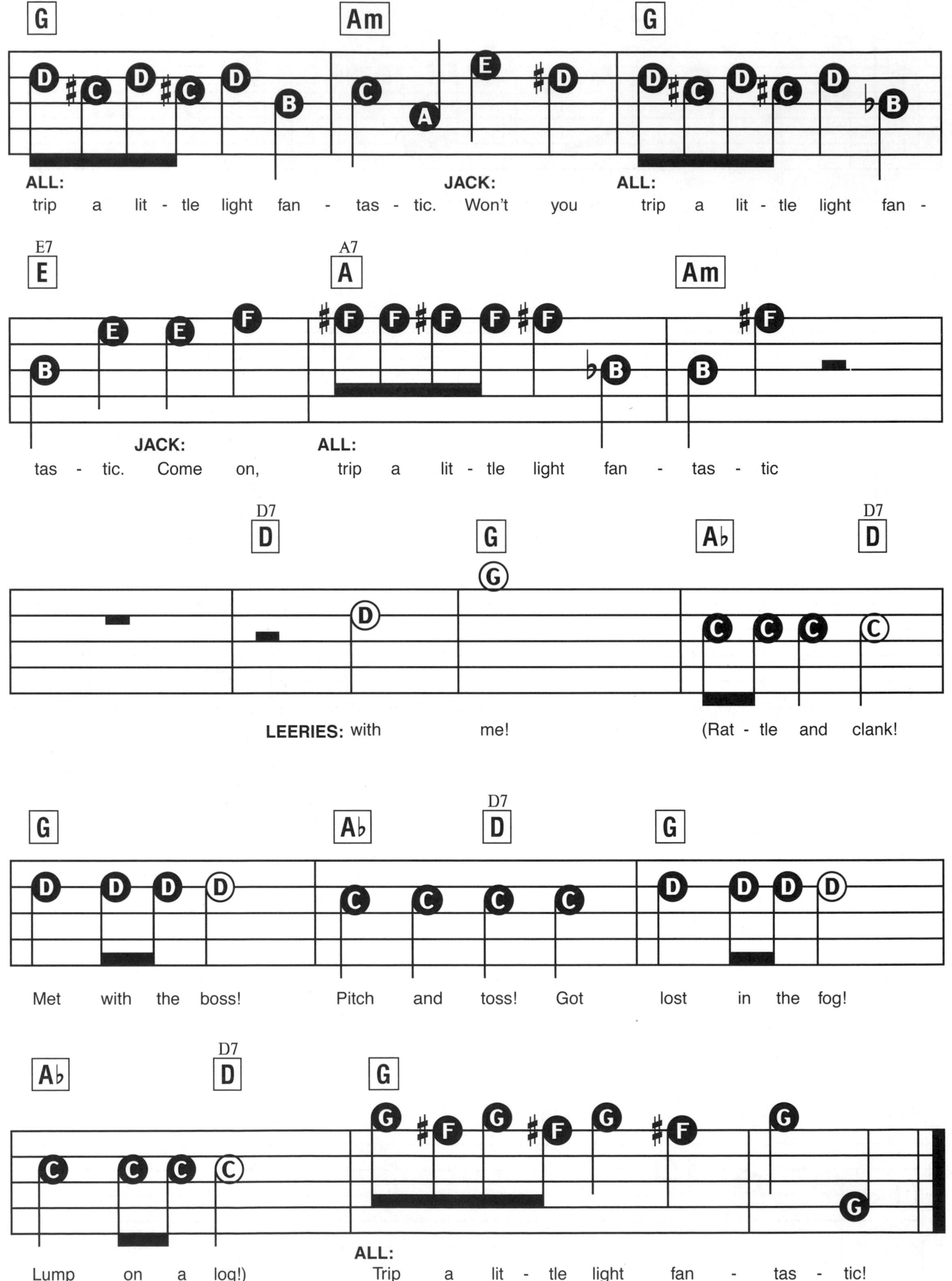
G Am G
ALL: trip a lit - tle light fan - tas - tic. JACK: Won't you ALL: trip a lit - tle light fan -
E7 E A7 A Am
tas - tic. JACK: Come on, ALL: trip a lit - tle light fan - tas - tic
D7 D G A♭ D7 D
LEERIES: with me! (Rat - tle and clank!
G A♭ D7 D G
Met with the boss! Pitch and toss! Got lost in the fog!
A♭ D7 D G
Lump on a log!) ALL: Trip a lit - tle light fan - tas - tic!